Reinventing the Welfare State

FireWorks

Series editors:

Gargi Bhattacharyya, Professor of Sociology,
University of East London

Anitra Nelson, Associate Professor, Honorary Principal Fellow,
Melbourne Sustainable Society Institute, University of
Melbourne

Wilf Sullivan, Race Equality Office, Trade Union Congress

Also available

Exploring Degrowth:
A Critical Guide
Vincent Liegey and Anitra Nelson

Pandemic Solidarity:
Mutual Aid during the Coronavirus Crisis
Edited by Marina Sitrin and Colectiva Sembrar

Fireworks

Reinventing the Welfare State

Digital Platforms and Public Policies

Ursula Huws

First published 2020 by Pluto Press
345 Archway Road, London N6 5AA

www.plutobooks.com

Copyright © Ursula Huws 2020

The right of Ursula Huws to be identified as the author of this work
has been asserted in accordance with the Copyright, Designs and
Patents Act 1988.

British Library Cataloguing in Publication Data
A catalogue record for this book is available from the British Library

ISBN	978 0 7453 4183 5	Hardback
ISBN	978 0 7453 4184 2	Paperback
ISBN	978 1 7868 0708 3	PDF eBook
ISBN	978 1 7868 0710 6	Kindle eBook
ISBN	978 1 7868 0709 0	EPUB eBook

Typeset by Stanford DTP Services, Northampton, England

To our grandchildren, in the hope that
they will grow up in a better world

Contents

Series Preface

Addressing urgent questions about how to make a just and sustainable world, the Fireworks series throws a new light on contemporary movements, crises and challenges. Each book is written to extend the popular imagination and unmake dominant framings of key issues.

Launched in 2020, the series offers guides to matters of social equity, justice and environmental sustainability. FireWorks books provide short, accessible and authoritative commentaries that illuminate underground political currents or marginalised voices, and highlight political thought and writing that exists substantially in languages other than English. Their authors seek to ignite key debates for twenty-first-century politics, economics and society.

FireWorks books do not assume specialist knowledge, but offer up-to-date and well-researched overviews for a wide range of politically aware readers. They provide an opportunity to go deeper into a subject than is possible in current news and online media, but are still short enough to be read in a few hours.

In these fast-changing times, these books provide snappy and thought-provoking interventions on complex political issues. As times get dark, FireWorks offer a flash of light to reveal the broader social landscape and economic structures that form our political moment.

Preface

The first draft of this book was written in a great hurry in the summer of 2019. I had recently finished a major research project on the extent and characteristics of platform labour in Europe, the results of which seemed to me to have profound implications for the future of employment and to confirm earlier doubts about the viability of the social model that has underpinned European welfare states since the Second World War. Even more broadly, the findings also raised questions about the organisation of daily life in the digital age. In combination, such questions opened up major concerns about the future of the welfare state, both in relation to its ability to provide safety nets for the vulnerable, promote equality and manage redistribution, and in relation to the kinds of services it provides to citizens and how they are delivered. I wanted to share these concerns with a wider audience, in the hope of contributing to a broad-based dialogue about how they could be addressed by public policies.

At that moment, British politics were in turmoil, dominated by divisive debates about Brexit. It seemed very likely that a general election was imminent, and with it a writing of manifestos and an opening up of discussions about what sort of society British people might want to inhabit in the future. It seemed an opportune moment to contribute to these conversations, enabling them to be informed by some of the results of this research. There was a risk, I thought, that some socialist policies, in seeking to reverse the effects of austerity and move towards a more equal society, might be aiming for a 'return to the 1970s', or even a 'return to 1945', which would fail to address the very real social and economic challenges of a digital global economy and the breakdown of solidarities between labour market 'insiders' and 'outsiders' that my work had uncovered. There was also a need to avoid idealising the twentieth-century welfare state, with its many imperfections. Especially, it was imperative that ways could be found to integrate feminist and green demands with more traditional social democratic ones.

At a time when much alternative public discourse was drowned out by the simplistic cacophony of 'Let's get Brexit done', how could dialogues be opened up in which such large questions about the future could be discussed seriously and constructively in a spirit of trying to find solutions that would meet the interests of a range of different groups?

Although the polarised political landscape, and media bias, posed formidable obstacles, it seemed to me that the best chance of building a consensus about how the welfare state could be reinvented would be to focus discussions around specific ideas for new initiatives. Perhaps people could be brought together to brainstorm creatively about ways in which the platform technologies I had been studying could be used to reorganise existing services and develop new ones, bringing into being a digital welfare state for the twenty-first century. At least the context of a general election put some of the relevant questions on the table with an urgency that was not present at other times. It seemed worth a try.

This was the original idea behind the book. But launching it in the middle of a snap election campaign in Britain entailed risks as well as opportunities. The UK first-past-the-post system mitigates against cross-party collaboration, and there is also pressure on each party to produce a precisely worded and fully costed manifesto that covers every aspect of government policy and inevitably takes a somewhat top-down form. At the very least, this sits in tension with any idea of building consensus around specific issues from the bottom up locally or regionally. At worst, it can throw up concrete barriers to any kind of collaboration, with each party trying to distinguish itself from its competitors by disparaging their policies.

In the event, these fears were academic. Thanks to a decision by the Scottish Nationalist and Liberal Democrat parties to break ranks with Labour and take Boris Johnson up on his challenge to go to the country to 'get Brexit done', the election was called even earlier than I had anticipated. Publishers' schedules were long and I had to undergo surgery in the autumn that put me out of action for several weeks as far as writing was concerned, so the upshot was that the publication of the book had to be delayed beyond the election period. My role in it was reduced to that of a voiceless bystander.

The Labour Party manifesto was comprehensive, ambitious and radical, touching on quite a few of the issues I wanted to address. Unfortunately, it did not receive anything like the detailed discussion it deserved in the rushed pre-Christmas tempo of the election campaign, overshadowed by the polarised debates over Brexit, and facing hostile media coverage. Although no doubt some elements from it will be adopted by a range of policymakers as the months and years go by, while other elements might form the basis for future campaigns, it is unlikely that this innovative manifesto will resurface in the same form.

Nevertheless, there is still a need, perhaps more urgent than ever in light of the results of the election, for a serious debate about the future of the welfare state in the twenty-first century in the context of a digitalised global economy. The changing context includes new challenges to the nation state posed by the increasing volatility of international trading agreements in general and, in particular, by Brexit. In the UK it also includes a likelihood that the deterioration in employment protection and benefit coverage experienced under the previous coalition and Tory governments will continue to worsen and reach crisis point. Meanwhile the need to address the climate emergency has become ever more visibly urgent.

This book is intended as a contribution to this debate. It does not seek to be a manifesto. Nor does it seek to cover every aspect of government. Rather, it aims to provide a starting point for discussion, experimentation and the search for solutions. It is likely that many of these solutions will not take a top-down form and be implemented formally by central government, but will be more piecemeal and bottom-up, rooted in local political alliances between different stakeholders and enacted at a regional or city level. The book seeks to lay the groundwork for such discussions by offering an analysis of how the principles underlying the welfare state have unravelled over the past 70 years and what the impacts of this have been on employment, social protection and gender relations, and hence on solidarity, equality and inclusion. Drawing on recent research, it then suggests ways in which these trends might be reversed, including by developing positive uses of the digital technologies that are sometimes held to be part of the problem, rather than the solution.

This was how this preface stood in February 2020, when I completed the first draft. Since then the world has changed in even more dramatic ways with the emergence of the coronavirus pandemic. This has given a new urgency to the issues I address and added to their topicality. Several of the trends I discuss have increased exponentially during the lockdown period.

On the one hand we have huge numbers of people working remotely from their homes, in many cases subjected to new kinds of electronic surveillance and digital management. On the other, in order to cater to their needs, there has been an equally dramatic need for other workers (mostly low-paid, precarious and disproportionately black and from ethnic minorities, and also subjected to surveillance and digital management), to deliver them the goods and services they cannot fetch for themselves, transport them to and from the locations where they need to be treated in person and, at great risk to their own health, provide them with that physical treatment. As the NHS is reorganised to accommodate patients with the Covid-19 virus, a new bonanza is created for the outsourcing companies that get the contracts. As small high-street shops, restaurants and cafes are driven out of business, the large corporations that dominate online shopping and delivery services increase their market share. And huge profits are made by the companies, many of which pay no tax in the UK, that take a rent from the increased use of digital technologies.

Meanwhile, neoliberal governments have had to abandon their pretence that the market can take care of the management of the state, embarking on a series of public interventions unprecedented since the Second World War, in the process opening up a space for radical debates that would not have seemed possible even six months ago, and exploding the myth that 'there is no alternative'. The UK government has manifestly failed to develop coherent policies to address the spread of the virus, and its public support has plummeted since the 2019 general election. The crisis has thrown up a new interest in UBI and other radical alternatives to the present system.

Finally, in the vacuum left by government incompetence, communities have come together locally to develop their own solutions to support the vulnerable, discuss ideas about what reforms to campaign for, and organise demonstrations to express their outrage against racism. In the process new social models are being developed that prefigure what a more inclusive post-Covid society might look like. Some of these community experiments, such as schemes to distribute food and essential supplies, coordinated online, resemble the suggestions I make in the later chapters of this book, giving these discussions, I hope, added legitimacy and relevance. Ideas that seemed utopian in my first tentative draft now seem more realistic and achievable. I offer them here in the hope that readers will build on them and, in the uncharted future that lies before us, start to formulate the basis for a new kind of welfare state fit for the twenty-first century.

Acknowledgements

This book draws on a large body of research on the platform economy, including 14 national surveys carried out at the University of Hertfordshire and funded by the European Foundation for Progressive Studies (FEPS) and the trade union confederation UNI-Europa. In the UK, additional funding was provided by the Trades Union Congress (TUC). I would like to thank these bodies for their generous support. In particular, I would like to thank Justin Nogarede at FEPS, Aileen Koerfer at UNI-Europa and Kate Bell at the TUC for their always constructive and hands-on engagement with the project, and my colleagues Neil H. Spencer, Matthew Coates and Dag S. Syrdal at the University of Hertfordshire's Statistical Support Unit for their patient and painstaking analysis of the complex survey data. Their contributions have been invaluable, but they cannot be held responsible for the views expressed here, which are my own. The book also draws on some of my other recent published material, including the discussion paper *A New Bill of Workers' Rights for the 21st Century*, published by Compass (www.compassonline.org.uk), a blog post 'The key criticisms of basic income and how to overcome them', published by Open Democracy (https://neweconomics.opendemocracy.net), a contribution to *New Visions for Gender Equality 2019*, published by the Gender Equality Unit of the European Commission's Directorate General for Justice (https://ec.europa.eu), and a number of posts on my personal blog (https://ursula-huws.wordpress.com).

For helpful and constructive feedback on the first draft, I would like to thank Christine Evans-Pughe, Malcolm Torry, three anonymous reviewers and the perceptive members of the Dalston Socialist Book Club.

I must also acknowledge the support of many other wonderful people who looked after me physically during the period in which this book was written and without whom I would probably not be alive to complete it. They include osteopath Joyce Vetterlein, medical herbalist Andrew Chevallier, dentist Greg Gossayn, surgeon Will Rudge and his team at the Royal National Orthopaedic Hospital, surgeon Alistair Hunter and his team at the University College London Hospital, the accident and emergency team and the staff on Ward 7 at the Princess of Wales Hospital in Bridgend, Doctor Stephanie and the nursing team at the Whittington Hospital's Ambulatory Care Unit, A. Chisholm and J. Calder of the London Ambulance Service, Mahesh Chemists in Newington Green Road, who bring me my medications however busy they are, and last, but by no means least, the unfailingly efficient, caring and proactive staff of the Miller GP Practice in Highbury New Park. I thank them all from the bottom of my heart. These committed, hard-working people represent what is best about our existing welfare state and the values that must be carried forward into the future if its spirit is to live on.

CHAPTER ONE

Introduction

Since 2016, worrying fissures have opened within the British working class and among the political parties that purport to represent its interests. Many have responded to this situation by retreating into polarised positions or succumbing to deep and paralysing forms of depression that render them despairing or inactive. This book is written to try to counter such reactions, in the belief that, despite these painful divisions, there is much more that unites people than divides them. Above all, and against some of the evidence from the 2019 general election, it seems to me that among the British people there is a deep hunger, across a wide political spectrum, for a welfare state that genuinely cares for its citizens, in all their diversity, from cradle to grave. New evidence for this hunger has emerged during the coronavirus crisis, although as I write it is still too early to tell where this will lead. Despite the many temptations to scapegoat others for the deficiencies of the existing welfare state, or to give in to defeatism, I believe that there are large numbers of principled people out there with the courage and fundamental decency to set aside their differences and campaign to bring a better welfare state into being. I write, therefore, from a position of optimism, offering this book as a constructive contribution to the development of a manifesto for hope and a collaborative form of politics that can build an alternative future. We owe it to our children and grandchildren to provide them with an economic and social environment in which they do not have to pour their energies into scrabbling to survive but can live decent and fulfilling lives and focus their energies on tackling the huge challenges facing the planet. Let's give it our best shot.

It is clear that the welfare state we have in the UK is no longer fit for purpose. But what can be done about this? This is one of the greatest challenges facing us as we enter the third decade of the twenty-first century. Do we try to recreate the cosy world of the mid twentieth century, or do we need to design something new, for a digital, global era?

The mid twentieth-century welfare state plays a powerful role in the socialist imaginary. It not only provides the ancestry of many of our present institutions, creaking though some of them may be, but also represents an aspirational model. In Europe, especially, it is still regarded by many as the norm by which decency is measured, promising security, social solidarity, cradle-to-grave protection against penury, equality of opportunity and a vision of progress.

When asked what a 'proper job' looks like, most people would still point to the model, established after the Second World War, at least for a privileged minority, of full-time, permanent employment with regular working hours, with the risks of illness, disability or unemployment covered by national insurance, and a pension waiting at the end to provide for a happy retirement. Similarly, there is still widespread support for the idea that a decent society is one that provides enough shelter to ensure that nobody has to sleep on the street, and a welfare safety net that prevents starvation.

Many would still agree with Beveridge's memorable aim of eliminating the five 'giant evils' of squalor, ignorance, want, idleness, and disease. It was in this spirit that the post-war Attlee government gave us several of the foundational features of what most British people still regard as normative social rights: universal healthcare, universal secondary education and a national insurance system providing universal pensions, child benefit and freedom from destitution via a social safety net.

The generations brought up in the embrace of this welfare state, or at least the socialists among them, have watched its slow unravelling over the last four decades with horror, putting their political energies into trying to preserve what they can of it – demanding the renationalisation of what has been privatised, the re-regulation of what has been deregulated and the reinstatement of budgets that have been cut. They demand, in other words, a solution that appears to many to be a turning back of the clock. Existing government institutions are often such a taken-for-granted feature of the social landscape that it can be difficult for people of this baby-boomer generation to separate the specific features of those institutions from the social goals that inspired their design. Their experience of trying to defend these twentieth-century bodies during the long hard years between the rise of neoliberalism at the end of the 1970s and the financial crisis of 2008 has made them deeply suspicious of reform. But this may also have made it difficult for them to comprehend the extent to which a gap has grown up between those original social goals and the way these institutions now function. And perhaps these very experiences may have desensitised them to the views of younger generations, who have only ever seen the welfare state through the prism of neoliberalism.

For anybody who entered the labour market after 1990, the post-war world of work – dominated by male bread-winners in full-time permanent employment supporting dependent families – is almost inconceivable. The fall of the Berlin Wall marked the symbolic establishment of a new international division of labour in which the protected workforces of developed Western economies were increasingly challenged by the existence of a global reserve army of labour, accessed by transnational employers either by offshoring the work to low-wage economies or by making use of a precarious migrant workforce in their home countries. This created a scattered though interdependent workforce, organised in global value chains, often outside the scope of national citizenship and therefore excluded from welfare coverage or employment protection.

In this context, strategies to try to restore the post-war employment and welfare model might seem like trying to reassemble a Humpty Dumpty that was specific to its time and place, a Humpty Dumpty that, moreover, while viewed romantically through rose-tinted glasses by those whose lives were formed by it, might actually not even be seen as desirable by younger generations. In proposing to restore it, proponents of this strategy run the risk of being seen as old-fashioned and irrelevant, aligned with rigidity and bureaucracy, and positioned, like King Canute, as trying fruitlessly to stem the inevitable tide of progress and innovation.

Indeed, most 'woke' young people who have grown up in the early twenty-first century would, if transported back to the 1950s, probably feel themselves to be in a restrictive, class-bound, sexist, racist and homophobic hell, as well as lacking in any scope to pursue an interesting or creative career or exercise choice as a consumer. It is hard to imagine anything they would hate more in practice than a return to many of the features of everyday life in the mid twentieth century.

This book pleads for a different approach. Drawing on extensive research on changes in labour and welfare, it argues that what is needed now is not a nostalgic recreation of the institutional landscape of the post-war welfare state but a return to the principles that inspired it. Having identified these principles, it argues, a hard-headed analysis of the social realities of modern Britain should be carried out in order to see how these principles can best be applied to address the needs of the present population – a population that is very different in many respects from the one that had survived the Second World War, and that brought its memories of the hungry thirties to the ballot box when it voted for Clement Attlee in 1945. The context in which these principles must be applied is one in which work and consumption are increasingly organised in global markets by tax-evading multinational corporations, where digital technologies are used to extract value from a vast range of economic and social activities, where woman are as likely to be involved in paid employment as men, where home-lessness and poverty are rife, where an ageing population has increasingly desperate needs for health and social care, and where the shadow of irreversible climate change hangs like a pall over everything.

In my view it would be a grave mistake to try to turn the clock back. We have a historic opportunity to rethink from first principles what a welfare state fit for the twenty-first century could look like, and we owe it to the victims of neoliberal globalisation to give it our best shot. This demands something that is both more ambitious than attempting to recreate a patched-up version of the third quarter of the twentieth century (viewed through the rose-tinted glasses of the twenty-first), and more focused on the specific issues confronting the working class in a globalised digitalised economy.

To understand the nature of the challenge it is first necessary to appreciate the immensity of the transformation of the mid-twentieth-century welfare state that has taken place over the last seven decades.

In this book I first look, in chapter 2, at how the institutions of the welfare state have been transformed by a series of shifts and subterfuges from a means of improving living standards, increasing choice and redistributing wealth more equally across society to mechanisms for redistributing from the poor to the rich. Chapter 3 looks at changes in the labour market and how the twentieth-century standard employment model has been eroded, leading to widespread casualisation and the emergence of new forms of digitally managed precarious work. Chapter 4 outlines the changes that have taken place in the gender division of labour over the same period, thwarting many of the grand aims of 1970s feminism. It shows the way that developments in the welfare system and the labour market have interacted with each other to produce a vicious circle in which time poverty and financial poverty drive each other downward in a never-ending spiral, in ways that are highly detrimental to gender equality as well as to the quality of life, at work and at home.

The rest of the book looks at ways in which this vicious cycle might be reversed, and how policies can be developed that promote equality, choice and improved work-life balance, while also addressing some of the other major policy challenges facing us – including caring for an ageing population, developing local economies and tackling food and energy waste.

In chapter 5 I look at the mechanisms of redistribution and the underlying principles that must underpin such policies. I then go on to make some concrete suggestions: for a form of universal basic income that is genuinely redistributive (in chapter 6) and for a new charter of universal rights for workers (in chapter 7).

In conclusion, the book looks at the services that the welfare state provides, or should provide, to make these redistributive and egalitarian goals a reality. It focuses in particular on services which have the potential to be delivered via digital platforms, such as those involving transport, food delivery and the matching of supply and demand between workers and clients in services such as childcare and social care. It extends its scope beyond the services that have traditionally been delivered by the state to explore others, such as food distribution, that, if brought within the scope of democratic control, could contribute more broadly to the public good, creating decent jobs and improving work-life balance for both women and men, while also addressing some of the major environmental challenges facing us.

The book does not propose dogmatic solutions in relation to the scope of such services or how they should be organised. Rather it suggests a variety of different possible ways of delivering them, for example by integrated them into existing institutions or setting them up as partnerships, social enterprises or co-operatives, with the aim of encouraging a bottom-up approach at local level rooted in collaboration among a wide range of different social actors.

CHAPTER TWO

What Has Happened to the Twentieth-century Welfare State?

For those who did not live through it, and even among some who did, there is a real danger of romanticising life in Britain during the period following the Second World War. In reality, it had many downsides. It was pretty hellish if, for example, you were black, or gay or unfortunate enough to get pregnant without being married. Although new opportunities were undoubtedly opened up for some, working-class kids who got scholarships to university or women who aspired to be taken seriously as intellectuals often faced condescension and ridicule. Indeed, it was a reaction to such strait-jacketed constraint and bigotry that produced the social movements of the 1960s – for women's liberation, for civil rights, for gay rights, for a democratisation of universities – led by the first generation of products of this post-war welfare state.

THE MID-TWENTIETH-CENTURY WELFARE STATE: A CLUSTER OF CONTRADICTIONS

In retrospect, many of the demands raised by the radical '60s generation that made their way onto political platforms in the 1970s have been collapsed by idealistic thinkers on the left into a fuzzy unity with those of the 1940s and 1950s – a sort of composite idea of the good old days before neoliberalism, when a post-Keynesian welfare state is presumed to have constituted an agreed consensus of minimum standards, upon which further progress could be built. Such a view glosses over the extent to which the third quarter of the twentieth century was marked by internal tensions and contradictions, some of which harked back to older tensions within the volatile assemblage of ad-hoc coalitions that has made up the British labour movement over its long and turbulent history.

One example is the tension between those, represented in the nineteenth century by followers of Ruskin and William Morris, who thought work should be meaningful and socially productive, and those whose goal was to put in the fewest possible working hours for the greatest possible reward – debates which resurfaced in the 1970s in discussions about Workers' Alternative Plans and the Institute for Workers' Control.

That is only one example. Many other tensions can be identified relating to other issues. Take, for example, the debates about women's reproductive labour among second-wave feminists in the 1970s: Should domestic labour be socialised? Should there be 'wages for housework'? Or should we rely on social pressure for men to do their share of unpaid work in the home?

Similarly, there were fierce disagreements about nationalisation and the position of workers employed by the state or in nationalised industries. Should they be regarded simply as members of the working class, who should negotiate with their employers in exactly the same way as those who worked for private companies? Or did they occupy a special position in providing services to citizens not for profit but for what Marxists called the 'use value' of these services?[1]

Such examples could be multiplied. The deeper one looked at how the welfare state functioned, the more contradictions emerged and the more challenging it became to imagine solutions that could create a successful balance between democracy and efficiency.

POST-WAR CIRCUMSTANCES FORGED UNUSUAL SOLIDARITIES

The British welfare state was forged in very special circumstances. A population with vivid memories of the horrors of the 1930s depression and the risks and deprivations and losses of the war had got used to centralised planning and rationing. A capitalist class still largely made up of nationally based companies was unusually minded to make concessions to labour amid genuine fears that workers would otherwise turn to communism. The old divisions between organised workers and what Marxists call the 'reserve army' of labour were criss-crossed by bonds, if not of strong solidarity, then at least of some mutual understanding. People who had stood together in ration queues and fought alongside each other in the war could unite around some common aspirations, not least the desire for a Labour government. And, as that government's plans began to be realised, further commonalities could emerge, even between groups that had historically seen their interests as opposed. In many cases, the securely employed and the potentially unemployed lived on the same new council estates, had their vaccinations at the same clinics, sent their kids to the same schools, recovered from their illnesses in the same hospital wards and listened to the same radio programmes. Common experiences nurtured mutual understanding.

It was possible in such a climate for the trade unions that represented organised workers to support demands that went beyond the sectional interests of their own members and extend them to cover the whole population. Universality was a key feature of the Beveridgean model: universal pensions, universal social insurance, universal child benefit, universal health coverage and universal access to education. And it was possible for this universality (and corresponding unconditionality) to be supported at least in part by the trade unions because it was clearly seen as in the general interests of the whole working class for it to be so. This was not just a case of 'there but for the grace of God go I' on the part of organised labour but an understanding among organised workers that their best protection against being undercut by cheaper labour, or scab labour, lay in ensuring that this reserve army would never be so desperate as to be induced to take a job at a lower rate or cross a picket line.

There was thus a material basis for solidarity between organised labour and the unemployed, expressed in the policies of the Labour Party – a solidarity that took institutional form in the kinds of tripartite structures that still exist today in some European social democracies, based on the notion that it was possible to have employers' federations representing most national employers and trade unions representing most of the national workforce, in dialogue with each other and with the national government, hammering out national plans for national industries. This notion, however, presupposed that national states were sovereign, with the powers to discipline both corporations and individuals on their territories.

The welfare systems that were constructed in these negotiations were intended to be redistributive. Companies and individuals paid into a system from which everybody benefited, with the sick, the disabled, the elderly, the unemployed and households with children able to take out more than they put in. In general, the discourse referred to need, rather than 'scrounging'. It is wrong to over-sentimentalise this picture, however. Claimants were subjected to all sorts of petty humiliations by bureaucrats, and the system was far from perfect. Nevertheless, it represented an historically unprecedented – if still limited – redistribution from capital to labour, orchestrated by the state.

A REVERSAL IN THE DIRECTION OF REDISTRIBUTION

It is widely believed that the state institutions inherited from this period still play the same role. After all, don't we still have healthcare that is 'free at the point of delivery', child benefit, housing benefit and a form of guaranteed income for the unemployed (the latest version of which is Universal Credit)? And don't the statistics show that the amount of money spent on social security, health and pensions is higher than ever before?

Such a view fails to grasp the immensity of the changes that have taken place in the intervening period. The twenty-first-century welfare state, while still inhabiting the institutional carcass of that of the twentieth century, now has a fundamentally different character. Far from redistributing from the rich to the poor, or from capital to labour, it now acts a vehicle for its exact opposite: a redistribution from the poor to the rich, from labour to capital.

How can this be? To answer this question we need to look first at who is putting money into the system – the taxpayers – and then at who the beneficiaries are. Those who get their information from the tabloid press or from television shows such as *Saints and Scroungers* or *Benefits Street* might find it difficult to believe that the welfare system is not simply channelling money from 'hard-working taxpayers' to 'scroungers'. But in fact the pattern of contribution to government income has changed substantially. Less and less of this income is coming from corporations and the rich and more and more from VAT (Value Added Tax) and other indirect taxes. This shift has accelerated since the recession of 2008. A 2016 report from the Institute for Fiscal Studies found that 'there have been substantial reductions in revenues from personal income, capital and corporation taxes as a proportion of national income. This has been partially offset ... by more revenue from indirect taxes, driven almost entirely by the increase in the VAT rate to 20 per cent from April 2012.'[2] And, as Richard Murphy has demonstrated, the poorest households in the UK have both the highest overall tax burden and the highest VAT burden. Meanwhile, many large global corporations – including those that benefit from employing low-paid workers – pay no tax whatsoever in the UK.

So, the poor are contributing disproportionately to the pot of money that pays for public services and welfare benefits. But surely they are also the main beneficiaries? Wrong again. Neoliberal policies have in fact turned the welfare state inside out to such an extent that private companies and rich individuals benefit from it disproportionately. Where does the spending on housing benefit go? Much of it to private landlords. Where does the spending on health and education go? Much of it to development companies (under PFI[3] deals), pharmaceutical companies, privately run academy schools and the multinational companies such as SERCO and G4S that provide the public sector with outsourced services. A report from the Institute of Government estimated that in 2017–18 the UK government spent £284 billion (rising to £300 billion if academies are included) on buying goods and services from external suppliers, amounting to a third of all public sector expenditure.[4] Many of the companies that benefit from these government contracts pay little or no tax. Virgin Care Services, for example – which made £8 million profit from NHS contracts with a turnover of £200 million in 2017 – paid no corporation tax on these profits for the second year running.[5]

And what about tax credits, the antecedent of the Universal Credit currently being rolled out? These were introduced by the New Labour government in the 1990s with the aim of reducing poverty while avoiding disincentives to work, taking the form of a top-up to low wages to bring household incomes up to an agreed threshold for certain categories of worker, such as lone parents. It was estimated that by 2015 expenditure on these credits, which had originally cost £1.1 billion annually, had reached £30 billion per annum.[6] Since tax credits are paid as a top-up to low earnings they must, so the narrative goes, end up in the pockets of the poorest workers. But why are these workers' earnings so low? It is, surely, because their employers are paying them so little that they cannot survive without the top up. Which means that the subsidy is going, not to the underpaid workers, but to the cheapskate employers who refuse to pay them a subsistence income. In other words it is a direct subsidy from the state to the employers that pay low wages. To add insult to injury, many of these employers pay little or no tax on their profits. Amazon, for example, which in 2019 employed 27,500 people in the UK, paid only £220 million in direct taxes in the UK, despite its total revenues from doing business in the country amounting to £10 billion.[7] The previous year it was reported that Starbucks, another large employer in the UK, paid effectively only 2.8 per cent UK tax.[8]

A TWENTY-FIRST CENTURY WORKHOUSE WITHOUT WALLS

In this upside-down welfare state, in which the poor are subsidising the rich, what is the experience of being in need? The Beveridgean welfare state did not hold with idleness, but did seem to aim to provide some dignity and choice to welfare recipients for whom benefits were supposed to be an entitlement, not something to beg for, as they had been in the dark pre-war period. So deeply engrained is the notion of social progress, that few British people would imagine comparisons could be drawn between the twenty-first-century welfare state and the Victorian workhouse, where families were broken up and the poor forced to do menial labour in return for food and shelter. Yet, viewed objectively, the welfare state today has many more features in common with its nineteenth-century predecessor than with the comparatively humane mid-twentieth-century model than we should be comfortable with. Gone is the idea that unemployed people, having paid contributions into a national insurance scheme, have an unconditional right to their benefits for a specified period. Instead, as 'jobseekers', they are forced by savage sanctions (withdrawals of benefit) regimes into accepting whatever work is available, however low paid, or, if no such work is available, into unpaid 'work experience' – the twenty-first-century equivalent of picking oakum or breaking stones (with the welfare system, as we have seen, providing their employers with a hidden subsidy for the use of this labour). Once sanctioned, many are rendered destitute: forced to sleep on the street or use food banks to survive. Perhaps the main difference is that the Victorian workhouse would at least have provided them with a bowl of gruel, a dry bed and a roof over their heads.

The statistics are shocking. According to the Trussell Trust, the number of emergency food parcels delivered to people in crisis by food banks reached a record 823,145 in the six months between April and September 2019, a 23 per cent increase on the previous year. Among the recipients, 'one in five have no money coming in at all in the month before being referred for emergency food' and '94 per cent of people at food banks are destitute'.[9] The number of rough sleepers also reached a record high. Research commissioned by the Greater London Authority found 8,855 people sleeping rough in London between April 2018 and March 2019, of whom 62 per cent were sleeping rough for the first time.[10] In 2018, the Department for Work and Pensions admitted that between April 2013 and April 2018 over 21,000 people died while waiting for benefits.[11] Meanwhile, it was estimated that the number of children from working households growing up in poverty rose by 38 per cent from 2010 to 2018 – from an estimated one in five households to one in four.[12]

THE GLOBAL DIVISION OF LABOUR HAS FRACTURED SOLIDARITIES BETWEEN ORGANISED WORKERS AND THE 'RESERVE ARMY'

Meanwhile, what has happened to the fragile solidarity between organised labour and the precarious reserve army of labour whose interests are constantly pitched against each other by employers trying to get work done at the cheapest possible price? As already noted, in the post-war period there were specific circumstances that enabled such solidarity, rooted partly in shared experiences and culture and partly in proximity, which meant that the same workers might move in and out of the reserve army, or see other family members do so. Institutional mechanisms existed for developing broad common demands and negotiating them at a national level. But the neoliberal policies introduced in the intervening period have driven deep wedges between workers, helped by technological change. Since the fall of the Berlin Wall in 1989, few parts of the planet have remained beyond the scope of transnational corporations. The reserve army is now, by and large, made up of strangers.

A global reserve army has been created, rapidly expanding, equipped with a basic knowledge of at least one world language, generic technological skills and a smartphone, able to be summoned at short notice to carry out one of the increasingly standardised tasks required in the twenty-first-century economy. This reserve army can be accessed in two distinct, but overlapping, ways: by moving jobs offshore to low-wage countries, or by using migrant workers in the domestic economy. In either case, a disciplinary effect is exercised over better-paid, organised workers. Whether you are told that your job could be sent to India or China, or outsourced to a company that employs migrant workers, the impact is essentially the same: you are less likely to hold out for demands for improvement to your wages and working conditions. And you are also less likely to know the workers who could replace you, to have mechanisms to appeal to their solidarity, or to empathise with their situation.

It is a rational response, in such a situation, to demand that the union dues you pay are spent on protecting the wages and conditions of the paid-up members and resisting any attempt to dilute the workforce. If you have lost faith in the ability of social democratic parties to represent your interests, it is also, unfortunately, a rational response to turn your anger against those unknown foreign workers who are undercutting you, and enter the embrace of xen-ophobic populist parties offering the promise of a return to the certainties of the past. This might explain much of the appeal of Brexit, Trump, Le Pen, the Freedom Party of Austria and the Alternative for Germany Party, although it says a great deal for the trade unions across Europe that, on the whole, they have been able to resist such divisive-ness and continue to campaign against racism among their members.

To pose the problem in this way runs the risk of understating the complexity of the situation. The lack of solidarity between indigenous workers and foreign-based or foreign-born workers cannot be reduced simply to racism, although racism may often play a role in it. Once the mechanisms that were created, and reinforced, by solidarity between organised workers and the reserve army have been shattered, the resulting fracturing of the working class affects people of all origins. Many of the households in poverty, the users of food banks and the people sleeping rough on our streets are white people of British origin who have been failed by the social safety net. The global division of labour must therefore be seen as one precipitating factor among several that has brought us to this pass.

DEMONISATION OF 'SCROUNGERS', IMMIGRANTS AND OVERSEAS WORKERS

By these and other means, welfare systems have evolved into a disguised means of redistributing from labour to capital, not from capital to labour. And this reversal has been disguised in such a way that the blame for it is displaced along multiple dimensions. Most obviously it is displaced onto welfare claimants, seen as 'scroungers' taking scarce resources from 'hard-working taxpayers'. But it is also displaced onto overseas workers, seen as stealing jobs from British workers, and onto migrants, who, in addition to stealing jobs and undercutting wages are also often perceived as consuming public resources, such as housing, education and health, which should by rights belong to native workers. The search for groups to blame does not stop there, however. Another favourite target is the elderly, adding an intergenerational wedge to the other divisions forced into the working class – splintered not just by employment and citizenship status but also by age.

BLAMING THE BABY BOOMERS

The elderly form a large and growing portion of the UK population. There are nearly 12 million people aged 65 and over in the UK, of whom 5.4 million are aged 75 or over and 1.6 million 85 or over. The Office for National Statistics estimates that by 2066 there will be a further 8.6 million UK residents aged 65 or over, who will make up over a quarter (26 per cent) of the population.[13]

Life expectancy is, however, falling, in a reversal of a long-term trend. The Continuous Mortality Investigation revised its Mortality Projections Model in 2019 to predict that life expectancies at age 65 had fallen by around five months for both males and females, to 19.8 years and 22.4 years respectively,[14] a trend it is difficult not to attribute to austerity policies.

Small wonder, then, that the pension bill is a prime target for those wishing to cut public expenditure, despite the fact that pensions in the UK are low compared with other European countries, at £141 per week, compared with £507 in Germany, £304 in France and £513 in Spain.[15]

The 2010s saw a path being prepared for future cuts. Several interrelated themes have been visible in the popular discourse, but they add up to a general message that the current generation of retirees is privileged, and that these privileges are gained at the expense of other groups in the population, especially the young, including their own children.

One common theme is that the baby boomers' pensions are being paid for by those 'hard-working taxpayers' who featured so prominently in the rhetoric of New Labour as well as Tory government propagandists. This misrepresents the reality to quite a considerable extent. During the 1950s, 1960s and 1970s, when most of the current crop of pensioners entered the labour market, the UK pensions system was still as it had been established under the 1946 National Insurance Act: contributions were paid by those in work, and their employers, into a common pot from which unemployment benefit, sickness benefit, retirement benefit (pensions) and other benefits were paid. Pension coverage was not universal (married women and some self-employed workers were excluded from it), but the principle was that everyone contributed to a system from which everyone then benefited.

The baby boomers thus spent the first two, three or even four decades of their working lives contributing to the basic state pensions of the generation that preceded them. Some were, of course, also enrolled in employer-provided pension schemes which provided additional income in retirement, but by no means all (in the case of women working part-time and people working for small companies, only a very small proportion).

Over the ensuing decades a series of changes placed pension schemes more and more into the hands of private providers and shifted the logic from one whereby people currently working paid for the pensions of their elders concurrently drawing pensions, to one where working people paid for their own future pensions, a principle whose most recent formulation was in the Pensions Act of 2008, with its 'defined contribution' principle that whatever the 'job-holder' puts in he or she should then take out.

This is quite contrary to the principle 'to each according to need, from each according to ability' that underpins most socialists' idea of what a welfare state should be about. It also strays away from the idea that contributions into a common scheme should be obligatory, a principle which even Winston Churchill recognised as necessary (in relation to unemployment insurance) because if it were not compulsory for everyone to pay into the system then only the bad risks would take out such insurance, leading to the failure of the whole scheme.[16]

Baby boomers have, in other words, being *paying into the system* throughout their working lives, though it is only in the latter part of their working lives (and in the case of many women and self-employed people, hardly at all) that many have been paying into their own private pension pots. Contrast this with the companies who benefit from tax credits, many of which are registered in tax havens and pay little into the public purse.

A second common theme is that baby boomers, often portrayed as selfish squatters, have benefited disproportionately from the rise in house prices and are occupying high-value properties that would otherwise be available for young people to live in. Again, let us leave aside the obvious point that in many cases young people, in the form of the baby boomers' own children and grandchildren, are already living with them in these properties, albeit perhaps sometimes with all parties wishing that they had a bit more privacy and control of their living space. There are some other myths here that need debunking. A few facts about the history of housing in the UK may help. During the twentieth century, owner occupation of homes grew from 10 per cent to 68 per cent, with most of that increase taking place in the last four decades of the century (it actually fell between 1938 and 1951). A high proportion of the rented accommodation (a majority from the 1970s onwards) was in housing owned by local authorities or (from the 1980s) housing associations. In the twenty-first century these trends have reversed a little, with a resurgence in the role of private landlords, so that by the 2011 census the breakdown was: 7.2 million homes owned outright, 7.8 million owned with a mortgage, 4.2 million privately rented and 4.1 million socially rented (of which 2.2 million were from local authorities and 1.9 million from other social landlords).[17] Nearly 70 per cent of homes, therefore, require the payment of either rent or mortgage to secure ongoing occupation. If the residents cannot keep up the payments, they will be booted out.

The majority of baby boomers were brought up in rented accommodation and started their working lives paying rent. Some, but not all, switched to paying mortgages when they could afford to do so (often driven as much by fear that rents were becoming unaffordable as by the desire for the proverbial 'home of one's own'). Those who chose to acquire mortgages had to sacrifice a considerable chunk of their incomes to pay them off. (Let us not forget that for every pound of the purchase price of the property you pay off with your mortgage you pay at least as much again to the bank, building society or mortgage company that lent you the money to buy it with.) Except in a minority of cases where it was inherited, the property these baby boomers now own was thus anything but a windfall (except to the moneylenders). Like their pensions, it was paid for from the wages of a working lifetime.

It is certainly true that many of these properties, including the former public housing that tenants were encouraged to buy from the 1980s onwards, have increased enormously in value. But let us look at what precisely was going on when the Thatcher government decided to sell off the cream of Britain's public housing stock. First, the cost of most this housing had *already been amortised*: the initial cost of building it had already been recovered. If the logic of the spirit in which welfare states were ostensibly set up had been followed, the rents of these publicly owned homes should have been very low. If there was no need to make a profit from them, all that the local authorities who owned them should have needed by way of income was enough money to cover the costs of maintenance and repairs and a contribution towards the cost of building additional new housing. So the tenants to whom these homes were sold off were in effect being asked to buy something that was already publicly owned and paid for. And since they had to get a mortgage in order to do so, half of what they paid was in effect a gift (in the form of interest payments) to the financial services companies that were such strong supporters of the Thatcher government, as well as beneficiaries from its policies.

But surely, readers might think, the people who bought these properties nevertheless benefited hugely from doing so, didn't they? Well, perhaps some did. But it is interesting how many people who were not former tenants did so even more. A surprisingly high proportion of former council flats have ended up in the ownership of private 'buy to let' landlords, including a number of Tory MPs (most notoriously Richard Benyon who purportedly collects £625,000 per year in tenants' housing benefits[18]).

But even when, after years of paying off their mortgages, people have managed to remain in possession of their properties, do they really get to leave them to their children as the enticing promises led them to believe? The answer is only yes if they are fortunate enough to die suddenly. Because of the pernicious distinction that has been drawn in the neoliberal welfare state between 'treatment' (which, although increasingly narrowly defined, is still provided free by the NHS) and 'care' (which most emphatically is not), the chances are very high that the house will have to be sold off, either before or after death, to pay for the rocketing costs of social care – provided by private companies which, in a further irony, are very likely to be employing workers on such low wages that they require tax credits to survive, and which may or may not be paying corporation tax.

So much for the baby boomers who scrimped and saved to pay off their mortgages. What of those who remained in their social housing and paid rent instead? Well they have been punished in another way – by the 'bedroom tax' introduced in 2013, whereby tenants' benefits are cut by 14 per cent if they have one spare bedroom and by 25 per cent if they have two or more. In other words, if they have any spare space whatsoever apart from their own bedroom (whether used to house medical equipment, a study or for any other purpose) then they have to pay an unaffordable extra sum of rent for it. So, although they may have faithfully paid rent for many years and put money and effort into maintaining and caring for the property, they are no more secure in their housing than anyone else.

GENERATION SET AGAINST GENERATION

What, meanwhile, has been the experience of younger generations? Let's look at the generation born in the early 1980s, now approaching their forties, too young to benefit from the advantages conferred by the post-war welfare state and too old to benefit from the softening of the Thatcherite policies introduced under the New Labour government of the 1990s. They were born too late, for example, for their parents to take advantage of the more generous funding for state nurseries in the pre-Thatcher era but too early to benefit from tax-deductible childcare costs and the Sure Start Programme. Their childhood was played out against a background of progressive cuts. Every year, something was withdrawn that had been available to older children, such as free music lessons, school trips or bus passes for travel to secondary school. They were the guinea-pig generation for much experimental governmental interference in schools, such as SATS examinations and the National Curriculum, and if they went to university they were denied the possibility of being subsidised by a local authority grant and were then hit with the requirement to pay tuition fees as well.

Not only did this generation suffer right through their education; once educated, they also entered a labour market in which the concept of a job for life had vanished. Apart from a lucky few, there were no apprenticeships or protected graduate trainee positions to be applied for. Suddenly, they had to compete, not just with the contemporaries they had been schooled with, but in a global labour market, with similarly qualified workers from all over the world. Without experience it was almost impossible to secure a decent job, and without employment it was impossible to demonstrate experience. The only solution to this Catch 22 on offer to the majority was 'work experience' – an unpaid internship that was supposed to confer 'employability' (in the process further undermining wages and conditions for the lucky workers who were actually paid).

The punishment of this squeezed and neglected generation, now in middle life, was also, of course, a punishment for their baby-boomer parents, though the young were encouraged to think of their elders as a privileged generation with interests opposed to theirs, on the one hand blocking the career ladder for ambitious juniors at work, on the other, a demographic time-bomb representing an unsustainable cost to the state and an impossible burden on younger generations.

CONCLUSION

We can conclude that, in the six decades since its establishment, the post-war welfare state has been transformed in character from one that, albeit to a limited extent, achieved a modest redistribution from capital to labour and provided a universal set of social protections, to its opposite: a state that redistributes wealth from labour to capital and, far from providing a safety net for its most vulnerable citizens, actually drives them into destitution if they fail to conform to its increasingly punitive terms. This transformation has been achieved under cover of an ideological subterfuge, with blame for misfortune being deflected onto other workers, or other groupings within an increasingly fractured working class. Different sections of the population have been played off against each other, while corporate interests have been rendered invisible, with the institutions of the welfare state playing a crucial role in the hidden transfer of wealth from the poor to the rich.

If we are to envisage positive ways forward, there is a need to look beyond these institutions and take a long hard look at what has actually happened in the labour market. Is it still even appropriate to think in terms of a 'core' workforce of organised workers and a peripheral army of casual workers waiting to take their place? This question is addressed in the next chapter.

CHAPTER THREE

What Has Happened in the Labour Market?

In the last chapter I suggested that the development of a global division of labour played a major part in breaking down solidarities among workers. This chapter looks in more detail at the breakdown of the normative model of employment that underpinned the mid-twentieth-century welfare state.

THE STANDARD EMPLOYMENT MODEL WAS ALWAYS INCOMPLETE

What is this model? In essence, while there were always exceptions, it assumed that workers worked full-time for a set number of hours per week (typically 40 spread over five days), with the weekend off and a certain number of days of paid holiday each year. Terms and conditions of employment were laid out in a letter of appointment which formed part of the legal basis of the contract of employment. Also specified were the worker's job title and duties and various other details, such as the rates at which overtime would be paid. National insurance contributions were levied, with contributions both from the employer and the employee, guaranteeing a certain level of benefits in return for working these standard hours. The worker was, for example, entitled to sick pay, holiday pay and, in the event of being made redundant, unemployment pay for a defined period, linked to length of service. The national insurance system also guaranteed workers a pension on reaching retirement age. Jobs defined as 'skilled' were generally considered to be jobs for life, for which workers were trained through apprenticeships or courses leading to recognised qualifications.

The model was predicated on the notion that the wages from this full-time permanent job would be sufficient to support not just the worker but also a dependent spouse and family. It aimed, in other words, to provide a 'family wage'. There were of course many cases where it did not stretch this far. Unskilled workers often earned much lower wages, including many immigrant workers from South Asia and the Caribbean who were recruited to work in the UK during the post-war period. Many jobs were casual, seasonal or involved working outside the 'normal' working hours of the five-day week, or away from the employer's premises. More importantly, in terms of the structure of the welfare state, the model also assumed a dependent wife working full-time as a housewife, carrying out care work and bringing up children supported by her husband's wage. This created incompatibilities between the time structures of the institutions offering services such as childcare, education and health and those governing working time. Unmarried women were generally expected to work until they were married, and then give up their jobs. In formally qualified sectors like teaching and the civil service, there were outright bans on married women working. In other sectors, such as banking and retail, a structure was normalised whereby young women were employed on lower grades, with lower pay, in the expectation that they would leave after a few years.

The model was thus never universal and began to break down with the growth in women's participation in the labour market, leading to a series of accommodations in the 1960s and 1970s including the formalisation of part-time working, the spread of temporary employment agencies and the introduction of maternity leave, equal pay and sex discrimination legislation. Nevertheless it continued to exert strong aspirational force as an idea of what jobs ought to look like, with part-time or temporary work described by policymakers and academics as 'atypical' or 'non-standard'.[1]

EROSION OF THE STANDARD MODEL

The erosion of the standard employment contract has not been total. The majority of UK workers are still on regular, permanent contracts. But there has nevertheless been a sharp rise in the number of workers on non-standard contracts, or, indeed, effectively no contracts at all, including precarious forms such as zero-hours contracts and temporary employment. The Office for National Statistics (ONS) estimated in 2019 that the percentage of people in employment on a zero-hours contract had grown from 0.6 per cent in 2010 to 2.7 per cent in 2019.[2] Temporary agency work was estimated in 2016 by the Resolution Foundation at 2.5 per cent of the workforce.[3] Furthermore, it was estimated that 4.2 million people were working from home in their main job in 2014 – the highest rate since comparable records began in 1998, when there were just 2.9 million. Of these, 1.5 million (5 per cent of those in work) worked within their own homes or its grounds, while the remaining 2.7 million (8.9 per cent of those in work) used their home as a base but worked in different places.[4] The ONS further estimated that the level of self-employment rose from 3.8 million to 4.6 million between 2008 and 2015, with a particularly strong increase in part-time self-employment (which grew by 88 per cent between 2001 and 2015), and with self-employed workers representing some 13 per cent of the workforce.[5]

Many of these self-employed people are defined as 'independent contractors' but lack the autonomy and choice that would render them genuine freelancers. Others are employed using tortuous devices such as 'umbrella contracts'[6] to evade restrictions imposed by employment law, immigration law or tax regulations. Some are the twenty-first-century equivalent of day labourers, plucked from a roadside queue to put in a few hours work on a building site, or waiting for a mobile phone alert from an online platform to summon them to perform a one-hour 'task'. Alongside and overlapping with these paid workers there is another even less easily quantified pool of unpaid people, mostly young, in internships or 'work experience' schemes, carrying out tasks that would have been paid in earlier periods, subsidised in various ways by parents, partners or the taxpayer.

THE EMERGENCE OF THE ONLINE PLATFORM

During the period following the 2008 crisis, several trends that had been bubbling under the surface reached critical mass and emerged into visibility. A global reserve army of workers, skilled in the use of IT and speaking global languages, had grown up during the 1990s to supply a range of services in fields such as call centres, IT support, data entry and legal and financial processing. What was distinctive about this type of work was that it could be carried out remotely, using telecommunications networks to transmit the work in a practice often referred to as 'offshore outsourcing'. My research in 18 European countries found that in 2000, 43 per cent of employers were engaged in some form of outsourcing using electronic links, while 6.8 per cent had employees working in remote back offices. The majority of this was in the same country or region, but no less than 5.3 per cent of establishments (more than one in 20) were already outsourcing digitally enabled services to companies in another country.[7]

At first, this source of cheap labour could only be accessed by large companies, able to cover the transaction costs involved in sourcing, recruitment, training and management of a remote workforce. But around the turn of the millennium a new business model emerged, exemplified in companies such as Elance, founded in 1999, Odesk, founded in 2003 (these two companies merged in 2013, and were rebranded in 2015 to form Upwork) and Amazon Mechanical Turk, founded in 2005. These companies, or online platforms as they became known, acted as intermediaries, linking workers with clients without the need for any advance investment by these clients, who simply paid a fee for each transaction. By eliminating transaction costs, the scope for using a global workforce for digitalised tasks was greatly expanded, bringing it within the reach of small firms or even individuals, a trend that was facilitated by the proliferation of devices such as smartphones, tablets and laptops and the Wi-Fi networks that made it possible to access the internet from ever more locations. The same model, allowing supply and demand to be connected quickly in real time in return for a fee, began to be used in the immediate aftermath of the financial crisis, by firms such as TaskRabbit and Airbnb (both founded in 2008) and Uber (founded in 2009), to make it possible to profit from supplying physical real-time services without having to invest in depreciating assets such as fleets of cars or hotels.[8]

In 2016, along with colleagues from the University of Hertfordshire, I carried out a survey of the UK workforce to investigate the extent of the use of online platforms for obtaining work and the characteristics of the workers doing this kind of work. The survey, funded by the European Foundation for Progressive Studies (FEPS) and the trade union confederation UNI-Europa, was followed up in 2019 by a second survey, this time with additional co-funding from the Trades Union Congress (TUC), to see what had changed in the meanwhile. The results were dramatic, showing an explosive growth in platform labour over the three-year period.

The number of people in the UK who said they did work obtained via an online platform at least once a week doubled from an estimated 2.8 million people to an estimated 5.8 million (from 4.7 per cent to 9.6 per cent of the adult population) between 2016 and 2019. For the vast majority, this was not a 'job' but a top-up to earnings from other sources. People were turning to the internet to make money in other ways too: over the same period the proportion of people renting out rooms via online platforms such as Airbnb went up from 8.2 per cent to 18.7 per cent, while those selling self-made products via platforms like Etsy rose from 10 per cent to 20.2 per cent. The main driver appeared to be poverty. During a period when earnings were falling in real terms or, at best, stagnating, and austerity policies had been biting hard, people were looking for any source of income they could find to make ends meet.[9] One of the most important mechanisms for doing this before the financial crisis – credit – was much less readily available, making the online economy an increasingly important resource to tap into.

Our parallel surveys in twelve other European countries showed a similar picture. Platform work is at its highest where earnings are at their lowest, with particularly strong concentrations in regions where there is a large informal economy. Platform work represents less than 10 per cent of all income for the largest group of platform workers in all countries, with only a small minority saying that it constitutes all their income. For most, it is therefore a top-up to other earnings and forms part of a spectrum of casual, on-call work in the daily lives of the working poor. Most report doing more than one kind of platform work. Those doing driving or delivery work range from 1.4 per cent (in the Netherlands and Sweden) to 12.3 per cent (in Czechia) of the adult population, but in the UK (the only country for which we have trend data) this proportion increased from 1.5 per cent to 5.1 per cent between 2016 and 2019, showing how rapidly it is growing. In every country the proportion doing driving and delivery work is exceeded by those doing more hidden types of platform work providing household services in other people's homes. This ranges from 2.4 per cent in Sweden to 11.8 per cent in Czechia. But this is exceeded by an even more common type of platform work – work that is carried out virtually, using online means. Consistent with the fact that such work is normally obtained via global platforms, it is unsurprising that by far the highest levels of online platform work are found in countries where average earnings are relatively low compared with international competitors, with the highest levels among our 13 countries in Czechia (at 23.5 per cent), followed by Slovenia (at 15 per cent), Spain (at 14.2 per cent) and Italy (at 10.4 per cent).[10]

This has brought about a situation where, if you are desperate enough for extra income, all you need is a smartphone or laptop and some basic tools of the trade, and – if your thumb is poised over the button to 'accept' a task quickly enough – you can augment your income by cleaning somebody's house, using your bike or scooter to deliver a package or a pizza, posting fake product reviews online, proof-reading somebody's PhD or a myriad other platform-mediated tasks.

A GENERAL 'PLATFORMISATION' OF WORK

Many of the practices of the online platforms date from earlier forms of digital organisation that have been with us for decades. For example it was common in the 1990s for supermarkets to use systems that enabled workers to be summoned at short notice to work a particular shift at a particular checkout. Similar practices, often using on-call or zero-hours contracts, were used in other services industries, such as pub or coffee-shop chains, warehouses and call centres, to bring in workers in response to fluctuations in demand – a 'flexibility' that was profitable for the employers but left workers unable to plan their childcare, their future spending, their holidays or other aspects of their lives. Platform work does not just mesh with other forms of precarious work organisation; it is also part of a broader process whereby digital forms of management are taken for granted. These are now gathering pace.

Our surveys found that digital organisational and management practices are widespread. The use of 'apps' to be notified of new tasks or record one's working hours extends well beyond the scope of online platforms. In 2016 one UK adult in ten reported using an app or website to be informed of new tasks but by 2019 this had more than doubled to 21 per cent of the adult working-age population. Barely half of these workers were platform workers. The use of apps or websites to record work done rose over the same period from 14.2 per cent to 24.6 per cent. Again, a majority reporting these practices were *not* platform workers. Nearly a quarter (24 per cent) of adults surveyed also reported having their work rated by customers, of whom nearly half (11.7 per cent) were *not* platform workers.[11]

These are symptoms of a much broader change sweeping across the labour market: the emergence of forms of work organisation in which workers are increasingly likely to communicate with their employers or clients via digital interfaces. This implies a loss of the direct face-to-face contact with a line manager that characterised most traditional forms of work, bringing with it an inability to negotiate directly and a loss of worker voice. Inserting a digital interface between the worker and the manager strips away the last vestiges of humanity from 'human resources management'. What work should be carried out and how it should be performed is dictated impersonally in a take-it-or-leave-it manner. As tasks become more standardised and their performance more likely to be monitored or recorded digitally (sometimes augmented by spatial tracking, using GSM), it becomes easier and easier to collect data on every detail of workers' performance. This in turn makes it possible to set targets and assess workers on how well they meet these targets. User ratings become part of the larger data sets that are drawn on in these new forms of algorithmic evaluation. And the more data is generated, the more sophisticated these processes become, in a vicious cycle whereby digital management breeds further standardisation, more precise targets and further digital management.

The underlying standardisation of work processes is not new. Standardisation is part of the long-standing logic that has made it possible to outsource and relocate work in the extension of global value chains that has been taking place for decades, as well as in the management of public services, making them fit to be outsourced to private companies for profit. Having to work to targets is now part of the common experience of a wide range of workers, from teachers to managers, from call-centre workers to chambermaids, from graphic designers to taxi drivers.

As these practices spread and become normalised, they become integrated with other aspects of work that are also increasingly taken for granted. One of these is the expectation that workers will be available round the clock to check their emails or deal with urgent communications from employers or clients. Another is that they will learn to use a range of standard online procedures to access services that previously would have been provided by a professional (ranging from booking travel to applying for a training course). Associated with these practices is the pernicious reality that workers are only ever as good as their last rating, and must 'pitch' for every new opportunity, whether this is a promotion, inclusion in a team or, if they are self-employed, a new task. The use of external ratings by customers puts the assessment of the quality of their work in the hands of strangers in a process that is not only deprofessionalising but also prone to bias. There is evidence, for example that female lecturers get lower ratings than male ones,[12] and black Uber drivers lower ratings than white ones.[13]

It could be argued that a new model of work is emerging, in which workers are increasingly required to be available on demand, managed digitally and expected to subordinate their own needs unquestioningly to those of customers or clients, carrying out work that has been reduced to standardised, measurable tasks. This is a workforce where there is a growing mismatch between workers' qualifications and skills and what they actually do to earn a living: where arts graduates work in coffee bars, economists with doctoral degrees drive taxis, nurses top up their incomes doing evening bar work and skilled production workers stack shelves in supermarkets. Coherent occupational identities dissolve in the construction of curriculum vitae made up of pick-and-mix assemblages of increasingly generic competences, evaluated by star ratings awarded by strangers.

Especially for young people habituated to measuring their self-worth by 'likes' on social media, taught by television talent shows that 'there can only be one winner' and that judges' decisions are unchallengeable, the competitive logic of this marketplace is hard to resist. In the repeated rejections that are an essential part of this process, there is a continuous battering of self-esteem that, especially in a context of insecurity and disentitlement, takes a heavy toll. Even when workers are organised and have permanent contracts, pressures to meet performance targets lead to stress and unpaid overtime and have been associated with high rates of mental illness in some professions, such as academic work.[14] When confronted with evidence that customers (students, in the case of universities, patients in the case of hospitals, callers in the case of call centres, passengers in the case of transport work) have given service workers a poor rating it can be difficult even for established trade unions to defend those workers strongly. Where work is carried out casually, or as a second job, the lack of representation and voice become acute.

REGULATION OF PLATFORM WORK?

The new model of work is one in which workers are increasingly atomised and disenfranchised while simultaneously, in an apparent paradox, being more tightly controlled and interconnected than at any previous time in history, thanks to digital technologies.

The platform or 'gig' economy has attracted considerable attention in recent years, with a rash of policy papers and a government enquiry, the Taylor Report,[15] published in July 2017. The usual approach is to regard platform work as a new kind of work, and platform workers as a new kind of worker. This often leads to a demand that they should be given a special status with special rights, differentiating them from other workers who are casual, self-employed or on-call. This approach somewhat misses the point because, as my research has shown, the vast majority of people doing platform work do not do it as a main job, and it is not their main source of income. Their primary identity is therefore not as platform workers but as something else, whether that is as a full-time, part-time or temporary worker, a freelancer, an agency worker or somebody deriving an income from a small business, rent or a pension. Any special status accorded to platform workers would thus miss a very high proportion of them.

More broadly, even if it could be applied to the small minority of workers for whom platforms *are* the main source of income, it would fall into the same trap as other narrowly focused efforts to control the casualisation of employment. Any attempt to develop specific responses to each new twist in employers' strategies for flexibilisation is doomed ultimately to fail. As fast as one loophole is closed, half a dozen more are opened. Furthermore, as well as absorbing a lot of energy and resources that could be devoted more productively to broader demands, this strategy places workers' organisations permanently on the defensive, responding, always several paces behind, to initiatives that have come from the employer and (because the rational response to deregulation is almost invariably a demand for reregulation) lining them up in the public perception as on the side of bureaucracy, inefficiency, control and inflexibility – sitting targets for anyone wanting to brand them as outdated and irrelevant.

Attempts to introduce blanket controls over specific forms of casualisation also run the risk of alienating some groups of workers. The self-employed, temporary workers, platform workers, part-timers or teleworkers are not unitary categories but contain within them many diverse occupational groups whose interests are not identical. For example a demand that homeworkers should have the right to employee status might gain the support of home-based clothing workers or data-entry clerks but be fiercely opposed by home-based journalists or IT consultants, whose freelance status actually gives them some bargaining power based on reputation and skill.

Perhaps unsurprisingly, the idea of creating a special status for platform workers was the approach that was adopted in the Taylor Report. As might be expected from a lead author who was appointed head of Tony Blair's Number 10 Policy Unit in 2005, this report is not short on spin. It speaks repeatedly of 'enduring principles of fairness', nods often to the idea of good work as an essential ingredient of happiness and well-being and claims to be focusing 'not just on new forms of labour such as gig work but on good work in general'. Pious mission statements, such as 'We believe work should provide us all with the opportunity to fulfil our own needs and potential in ways that suit our situations throughout our lives', sit alongside references to the inevitability (and benignity) of technological progress. In the classic contradictory neoliberal formula, it manages simultaneously to say that 'Good work is something for which Government needs to be held accountable' and 'The best way to achieve better work is not national regulation but responsible corporate governance.'[16] It is perhaps noteworthy that Taylor's co-investigator, Greg Marsh, was a former investor in that most visible of gig economy companies, Deliveroo.[17]

The report quite rightly recognises that the employment status of casual workers is confusing and poorly understood. This is partly because it is dealt with separately under the tax system and in employment law. Under the tax system, unless you have some other legal status such as being a limited company or a partnership, you are either an employee or self-employed. Many workers living hand-to-mouth think it is preferable to be self-employed because that way they can defer the payment of income tax and set expenses against it. Under employment law, being an employee brings a range of rights and protections, including such things as maternity and paternity pay, sick pay, parental leave and pension coverage. These are probably worth much more to most workers in real terms than whatever tax savings they make by being self-employed, but of course can only be claimed if their employers actually agree that they are indeed employees and fulfil their part of the bargain. There are some rights guaranteed under employment law to all workers regardless of whether they are formally classed as employees, but few are aware of them. These include the right to the minimum wage and to paid public holidays.

The difficulty of establishing employee status is not new. Back in the 1970s and 1980s, when I was doing research on homeworking, this issue came up again and again. Frightened women, unaware of their rights, were told firmly that they were not employees (often believing – usually wrongly – that what they were doing was not quite legal and that if it were found out they would become liable for tax or national insurance payments or fined for being in breach of health and safety or tenancy regulations) so they would shrug and accept that they had no rights. The law had no single test for being 'genuinely self-employed'. Tribunals or courts were supposed to weigh up several different factors such as who determined what work should be done, what should be paid for it, whether the worker had the right to employ somebody else to do it, how continuous it was, who paid for the materials and so on. Little has changed since then, although the case law has moved on. The most crucial principle is whether a relationship of subordination can be said to apply.

In the case of most platform companies, there is little doubt that the workers are indeed subordinate. Although practices vary from company to company, workers are usually told precisely what to do, with each 'task' tightly defined and costed. Not only are their pay and work processes laid down, there are also usually detailed rules about quality standards. While there may be some limited right to turn a few jobs down, there are usually strong penalties for doing so repeatedly. Workers typically do not have the right to pass the work on to others. And in some cases they are even required to wear uniforms or sport company logos. They can be dropped from the platform without warning if, for example, their user ratings fall below a certain level.

The Taylor Report could have laid out clear guidelines for defining genuine self-employment and spelled out the obligations of employers of subordinate workers. But what it did instead was muddy the waters still further by proposing exceptions to the existing principles, exceptions which could be detrimental not only to workers who are currently working casually but also to other workers, including those currently defined as employees.

One main recommendation was the establishment of a new intermediate kind of employment status – 'an intermediate category covering casual, independent relationships, with a more limited set of key employment rights applying.'[18] This approach has been rightly resisted by British legislators in the past, and is not a particularly original response. Indeed, it something of a knee-jerk reaction by neoliberal 'modernisers' to the development of new forms of work. The overwhelming evidence is that when new kinds of status (such as the status of 'parasubordinate worker' in Italy) are established they do not just result in reduced protection for the 'new' kinds of workers who fall under them but, even more importantly, are then extended across the workforce to bring other more traditional groups of workers within their scope, resulting in a worsening of conditions across the board. In other words, what they do is provide employers with a new tool for casualisation and the erosion of existing rights, whatever well-intentioned language is used that purports to prevent this.

The Taylor Report also proposes a change in the way that the national minimum wage (NMW) is applied: 'In re-defining "dependent contractor" status, Government should adapt the piece rates legislation to ensure those working in the gig economy are still able to enjoy maximum flexibility whilst also being able to earn the NMW.'[19] What it proposes is complex. At the headline level it looks like a proposal to increase the NMW by a modest amount for workers with the proposed new 'dependent contractor' status. However, the report also wags a stern finger at those who think that workers should be paid for all the time they spend waiting for jobs to come up, which is, they say, unreasonable and open to abuse. Given that many workers in the gig economy spend half their time or more logging on in the hope of work that does not arrive, this could in practice lead to a fall in the time eligible for payment and hence take their earnings well below NMW rates.

The idea that platform workers represent a new category of worker distinct from the rest of the working class comes not only from policy advisors and think-tanks. It can also be found among sections of the left who, inspired by the ways in which some platform workers have begun to organise, have romanticised them as a new vanguard among precarious workers, part of an emerging movement that is developing new forms of resistance, organisation and representation and formulating new demands in an upsurge of grassroots activity perhaps unprecedented in Britain since the birth of general trade unionism in the 1880s.

NEW FORMS OF COLLECTIVE ORGANISATION AMONG CASUAL WORKERS

Since 2016 there has certainly been a growth in collective organisation among casual workers in the UK (and elsewhere). Traditional trade unions have made considerable advances in organising casualised and low-paid workers. Unite's Decent Work for All[20] campaign was an important initiative here. In 2017, the Bakers, Food and Allied Workers Union organised a strike at McDonald's (the first since the company opened in the UK in 1974), demanding a raised wage, more secure working hours and union recognition.[21] Several other unions have campaigned for the abolition of zero-hours contracts. Elsewhere, new trade union organisations, such as the ADCU (App Drivers and Couriers Union) and the IWGB (International Workers of Great Britain), have sprung up to represent drivers for platforms like Uber and delivery workers for companies like Deliveroo and City Sprint, as well as casualised workers in other sectors, such as outsourced cleaning workers, porters and foster carers. A series of test cases brought by these organisations and by traditional trade unions, like the GMB, have established in case after case that workers for companies like City Sprint, Uber and Pimlico Plumbers are not the 'independent contractors' these companies claimed they were but 'workers', entitled to such rights as the minimum wage and paid holidays. As a result of these and other well-publicised cases of exploitation of low-wage workers, such as at Sports Direct, there has been a sea-change in public attitudes to fairness at work, evidenced by the popularity of the demand for an end to zero-hour contracts in the Labour Party's manifesto for the 2017 general election and further developed in its manifesto for the 2019 one. This bodes well for future campaigns to improve workers' rights, discussed later in this book.

One archetypal worker who has attracted considerable attention and seems to symbolise this new movement more than any other in the popular imagination is the food delivery rider. Generally portrayed as a white male cyclist, this figure has become emblematic not just of the gig economy in general but also of the ways that workers are starting to organise against online platforms. There is indeed something heroic about the way that, in city after city around the world, these riders are coming together, taking part in colourful protests, joining trade unions, taking on the platforms in the courts and, in 2018, forming a new international organisation – the Transnational Courier Federation.[22] In these pessimistic times, what socialist does not rejoice at the thought that precarious workers really can organise, and want to partake vicariously in their successes? In January 2020, in an even more momentous development, driving workers from 23 countries met in the UK to set up the International Alliance of App-based Transport Workers,[23] opening up new possibilities for taking on global ride-share companies internationally. Surely, these workers are living proof that the spirit of trade unionism is not dead and that the impulses for solidarity and collaboration can resurface even in situations of extreme atomisation and competition between workers.

It would, however, be a mistake to assume that these two groups represent the majority of platform workers. What our research has shown is that, important though they are, they are far outnumbered by other platform workers, working in more hidden ways. The largest group is made up of people working remotely for online platforms like Upwork, Fiverr or Clickworker in global markets doing anything from low-skilled 'click work' to higher-qualified professional work such as software development, graphic design or editing. Then there is another significant group (also exceeding the driving and delivery workers) doing a variety of household work including cleaning, babysitting, assembling flat-pack furniture, plumbing, gardening, building and repair (for platforms like Helpling, Task-Rabbit, MyBuilder or Findababysitter). These groups are much harder to identify and organise.

It is perhaps not coincidental that drivers, like couriers, work in public spaces where they are able to identify each other, meet and organise, and part of the explanation for the focus on delivery and driving workers as typical platform workers seems to lie in this visibility – not just to random observers but also to each other – making it relatively easy for them to compare notes, discuss grievances and get together to formulate strategies to improve their situations.

They remind us of past struggles, like those of the East London dockers in the nineteenth century who organised to bring dignity and fairness to a situation described by their leader, Ben Tillot, in the following words 'We are driven into a shed, iron-barred from end to end, outside of which a foreman or contractor walks up and down with the air of a dealer in a cattle market, picking and choosing from a crowd of men, who, in their eagerness to obtain employment, trample each other underfoot, and where like beasts they fight for the chances of a day's work'[24] – a situation not all that different from that of platform workers who with equal desperation wait, thumb poised, to click 'accept' on a newly posted task before somebody else gets it. Who could not applaud these twenty-first-century equivalents of the casual dockers, with similar goals, exhibiting similar courage?

Those dockers, like today's delivery riders and taxi drivers, waited together in close physical proximity in the places where there was likely to be the greatest demand for their services; as a result, they were well placed to organise. And their efforts clearly brought results which, over time, became integrated into the institutional landscape, for example in the development of the National Dock Labour Scheme, or, in the not dissimilar case of the Licensed Taxi Drivers Association, led to agreements covering standard charges, licences, etc. This very success, of a type repeated across the labour movements of the world, might provoke in some a belief that this form of organisation is all that is needed. Whatever new form of work emerges, it may be thought, so long as the workers get together and follow the example of other trade unions, they will sooner or later be able to bargain their way into a situation that conforms ever more closely to the standard employment model. It is worth remembering that, although it undoubtedly would not have been established so decisively without the militancy of the dock workers, including a strike in 1945, the National Dock Labour Scheme was introduced by a

Labour government as part of a more general package of measures of nationalisation and regulation that we now, retrospectively, think of as part of the post-war welfare state. It is highly unlikely that it could have been achieved by collective bargaining alone.

THE LIMITS OF COLLECTIVE BARGAINING

Such forms of organisation among workers who meet each other face to face are obviously welcome. But what about all those workers who are not visibly present in public spaces, and who do not get a chance to meet in person? What about those who aren't even competing with compatriots but are bidding against competitors across the world in economies where wage levels, employment laws and working conditions are very different?

In late nineteenth-century London the dock workers managed to organise, as did some factory workers, including women. But there was very little organisation among the tens of thousands of domestic servants, skivvying away in private in other people's basements during the day and sleeping in their attics by night. Their twenty-first-century equivalents (such as individually employed cleaners, babysitters and care workers) are not usually provided with a bed, but are expected to work in equally hidden circumstances, under extremely tight time pressures, and with the constant threat hanging over them that a bad customer review might lead to them being dropped from the platform with no right of appeal. Domestic workers around the world have managed to organise effectively, from South Africa to Hong Kong to California, often against appalling odds. But the circumstances in which they work place huge obstacles in the way of their being able to identify and meet each other (very often, the only way for workers to contact one another is via ethnic or community-based organisations).

It is when we consider such vulnerable groups, often women, often migrant workers, that we come up against the limits of sector-based or occupation-based collective bargaining as narrowly conceived and, in the same spirit as the nineteenth- and twentieth-century trade unions, need to start campaigning for society-wide measures that cover all workers, regardless of whether they are signed-up members of particular unions. What is needed is not just the right of cycle couriers, for example, to have a particular employment status or a particular level of minimum pay, but generalised rights for *all* workers to have employment protection and a national minimum wage. Nevertheless, the mobilisation of those workers who *are* able to organise plays an important role in bringing these demands to public visibility and pushing policymakers to act. One of many historical examples of this is the pivotal role played by the 1968 strike for equal pay by women machinists at the Dagenham Ford factory in persuading a Labour government to pass the 1970 Equal Pay Act. There is often a synergistic relationship between collective action and the development of government policy.

The need for universal rights becomes even more apparent when we consider the general 'platformisation' of work that was also revealed by our surveys. Issues such as algorithmic management, performance targets, misuse of workers' personal data and the disciplinary use of customer ratings affect a wide range of workers across different occupations and sectors and call for an approach that establishes minimum standards that apply to everybody. Making rights universal for all workers across the labour market, like having a universal minimum wage, has several clear advantages. First and most obviously it can provide a floor below which standards cannot fall, making it more difficult for one group of workers to be played off against another. Second, if it is clear and easily understood by all it is much easier for workers to claim their rights. And third, if there are mechanisms for inspection and enforcement, the costs of taking legal action to test arcane details will be reduced substantially. Finally, the commonalities between organised workers and the reserve army of unemployed or casually employed workers can provide a basis for rebuilding solidarity between them.

CONCLUSION

This chapter started by looking at the standard employment model of the mid twentieth century, pointing to its limitations as well as its strengths. It then went on to document the slow unravelling of this model over the decades. This was partly triggered by the model's own limitations, in particular its failure to include women workers within its scope, but it was also undermined by the development of a global division of labour, facilitated by the use of computing and telecommunications technologies which enabled work to be relocated and remotely managed. This development, limited to large companies in the 1990s, has now been supplemented by the explosive development of online platforms. This has not only created new forms of easily accessed task-based work but has also been associated with a more general 'platformisation' of work across the economy, with a substitution of digital and algorithmic forms of management for direct face-to-face supervision of workers. I went on to summarise some of the debates about how these new forms of work might be regulated before going on to discuss new forms of organisation among casual and 'gig' workers. While these are to be welcomed, they do not offer a complete solution. What is needed is a new set of universal workers' rights appropriate for the twenty-first century. What some of these rights might look like is outlined in chapter 7.

POSTSCRIPT

Many of the trends described in this chapter accelerated sharply in 2020 in the context of the lockdown introduced by the government in its, rather delayed, response to the coronavirus epidemic, though some have gone – at least temporarily – into reverse.

Some of the negative economic shocks result from the sharp reduction in international travel and tourism during the pandemic. This has brought about financial ruin for many Airbnb hosts and companies in the travel sector.[25] Probably much more important in the long run, however, has been a massive extension of the use of online platforms for the delivery of a wide range of goods and services to consumers locked down in their homes, substituting digitally managed services for those formerly delivered directly by face-to-face means, and enabling large corporations to colonise huge areas of the economy formerly dominated by small firms and individual traders in the informal economy. The coronavirus crisis has made visible and accentuated an increasing polarisation across the labour market between 'fixed' and 'footloose' work and workers,[26] whereby the needs of those who are immobilised, whether through the constraints of the technical division of labour, incapacity, old age or the risk of contamination, are increasingly met through the hyper-mobility of other travelling workers who must deliver them the goods and services they cannot fetch for themselves, provide them with physical care, or transport them to and from the locations where they need to be treated in person.

It is one of the nastier contradictions of the neoliberal global market economy that these footloose workers, who, by a further twist of irony, are much more likely than average to be migrants or of black and ethnic minority origin, are exposed to the greatest risks while also being least likely to be protected by employment rights (including sick pay, job protection, minimum wages, etc.), while their personal safety is sacrificed for that of the rest of the population. During the coronavirus crisis, it looks very much as if their numbers are expanding enormously, with their ranks being swelled by workers made redundant from other sectors who are now subjected to the new disciplinary structures pioneered by global platforms.

In a parallel development, members of the 'fixed' workforce, confined to their homes under lockdown conditions, are increasingly required to work remotely, using digital links to their employers or, if they are self-employed, clients. There are reports, for example, of employers using always-on camcorders on workers' computers to take a picture every five minutes to monitor their presence at the screen in a ratcheting up of surveillance and an extension of the practices of online platforms across the labour market.[27] The isolation of home-based work not only makes collective organisation more difficult but also brings risks of mental and physical illness.[28]

Both these developments appear to be converting an exponentially growing portion of the workforce into 'logged' workers as well as dramatically extending the market share of global corporations across national economies. Combined with the new forms of state surveillance of the general population that are being legitimised by the need to monitor the spread of the Covid-19 virus, these trends are extending algorithmic control while bringing more and more areas of daily life under its direction. In an apparent paradox we are simultaneously seeing the development of new fault-lines in our fractured labour markets while new commonalities emerge among workers in 'fixed' and 'footloose' occupations.

The ways in which the virus spreads have also heightened public awareness of the disproportionate share of 'key workers' who are from black and ethnic minorities, and their increased risk of dying from exposure to it.[29]

These developments add weight to the argument that fundamental changes are needed, and bode well for the likelihood of increased public support for such changes.

CHAPTER FOUR

What Has Happened to Gender Equality?

The post-war welfare state was built on a highly asymmetrical model of gender relations. Although women had been drawn into the workforce in large numbers during the Second World War, there was a general expectation that when the men had returned to civilian life they would give up their jobs and retreat into the roles of mother and housewife, at least once they were married. Before marriage, women often worked in labour market ghettoes with few promotion prospects, and many industries developed employment patterns to accommodate this.

In banks, for example, the majority of tellers working behind the counter dealing directly with customers were young women. For the minority of men in these roles, a job as a teller was a stepping stone to promotion to becoming a manager, but for women it was a dead end. They were expected to leave when they were married, so what would be the point of training them for higher things? Wages for unskilled labour were too low to support a family, so many working-class households actually relied on women's work to top up their income, but this was often from unprotected low-status work such as 'charing' (casual cleaning work) or home-based sewing. Some factories developed 'mum's shifts' to enable women to do production-line work at hours that fitted in with the timetables of schools or their husbands' work.

School curricula reflected a strongly gendered occupational structure, with girls channelled towards secretarial work, teaching, nursing or hairdressing while their brothers were directed, varying by class, region or educational achievement, to a range of manual jobs involving physical strength (such as mining, farm labouring, driving or factory work), professions, technical occupations or managerial roles. This asymmetrical gender pattern not only characterised the education system but was reflected across a wide range of social institutions. Your gender did not just determine what sort of job you might get but also your pension, what benefits you were entitled to, whether you could get a mortgage or a bank loan or take out a tenancy agreement, and many other aspects of life.

THE TWENTIETH-CENTURY WELFARE STATE DID NOT TREAT MEN AND WOMEN EQUALLY

In short, in its first, Attleean version, the twentieth-century British welfare state cannot be regarded by any stretch of the imagination as one that was committed to gender equality. This is not to say that it was not concerned for women's well-being. It improved their lives immeasurably by providing decent maternity and healthcare, child benefit, pensions, housing and other services. However, it did so while regarding them as different from and complementary to men: mother, carers and helpmeets rather than independent fellow citizens with equal rights.

This picture changed dramatically in the 1960s when the first generation of children brought up in the welfare state reached adulthood. Several trends cross-fertilised to bring about a sea-change in public attitudes. Reforms to and expansion of higher education and the introduction of student grants made it possible for growing numbers of people from working-class backgrounds, including women, to go to university. Relatively full employment gave young people independent incomes and the wherewithal to buy some of the consumer goods newly available in rapidly expanding markets. The growth of the welfare state itself and of service industries such as retail, banking and tourism created new jobs for clerical and administrative staff, nurses, teachers and shop assistants, many of which were taken up by women. The introduction of the contraceptive pill combined with more liberal attitudes to pre-marital sex, illegitimacy and homosexuality to contribute to a reaction against the confining family model this generation had grown up with.

THE STRUGGLE FOR WOMEN'S LIBERATION

A sense of entitlement spread among women, leading, for example, to major strikes among female clothing workers in Leeds, car workers in East London and electronics workers in West London. The Women's Liberation Movement formed and, in 1970, formulated its first four key demands: for equal pay; equal education and job opportunities; free contraception and abortion on demand; and free 24-hour nurseries. Later, three further demands were added: for legal and financial independence for all women; the right to a self-defined sexuality and an end to discrimination against lesbians (in 1974); and (in 1978) freedom for all women from intimidation by the threat or use of violence or sexual coercion regardless of marital status and an end to the laws, assumptions and institutions which perpetuate male dominance and aggression towards women.

As in other countries during this period, the growing militancy among women, alongside movements against racism and for civil and trade union rights, led to a wave of legislation. The Race Relations Act (classifying some forms of discrimination as civil offenses) was passed in 1965 and strengthened in 1968. Abortion was legalised and homosexuality decriminalised in in 1967. The Sex Discrimination Act and the Equal Pay Act were passed in 1970, but did not actually come into effect until 1975, giving employers a five-year period in which they could 'prepare for the Act'. The Equal Pay Act established the right to equal pay: if 'the work done by the claimant is the same, or broadly the same, as the other employee'; if 'the work done by the claimant is of equal value (in terms of effort, skill, decision and similar demands) to that of the other employee'; or if 'the work done by the claimant is rated (by a job evaluation study) the same as that of the other employee'.[1] During the five-year preparatory period steps were taken to minimise the impact, creating a more clandestine form of segregation. For example, women and men doing similar jobs were shuffled apart or given different job titles and job descriptions (for example a female server in a café would be designated a 'waitress' and her male counterpart an 'assistant manager'), and numerous job evaluation studies were carried out in which work processes were analysed and points awarded for various different kinds of 'effort', 'skill' and so on, producing job profiles that gave a scientific legitimacy to a ranking that might, for example, award a (male) fork-lift truck driver in a factory a higher rating than a (female) skilled sewing-machine operator in the same factory. It thus became extremely difficult for a woman to find a male comparator in order to make a claim for equal pay.

FORMAL EQUALITY IN THE WORKPLACE

Nevertheless, the existence of these Acts led to a focus on equal pay and workplace discrimination as key indicators of progress towards gender equality. Later, considerable effort went into amending the Acts to try to make them more effective (for example by introducing the concept of 'work of equal value'), collecting statistics on the 'gender pay gap' and workplace segregation, and introducing targets for the representation of women (and other under-represented groups) in higher-valued occupations and management grades. Success was thus overwhelmingly measured by indicators related to paid participation in the labour market. This approach is typified in the following statement by the Equalities and Human Rights Commission, from 2017, in which no explicit mention is made of any structural factors outside the labour market and the educational system:

Across Great Britain in 2016 the gender pay gap stood at 18.1 per cent ... the ethnicity pay gap at 5.7 per cent

... and the disability pay gap at 13.6 per cent ... These average figures disguise wide differences, with some groups experiencing far greater pay gaps than others ... However, at their root are some common causes such as poorer educational attainment, different educational choices and the concentration of these groups in lower paid, lower skilled and part-time jobs.

Our research shows that the pay gaps experienced by women, people from ethnic minorities and disabled people arise largely from the barriers they face getting into and progressing at work.[2]

In such discussions, many of the issues raised in broader debates that took place among second-wave feminists in the 1970s have been downplayed, sidelined or forgotten.

In the UK, women's labour market participation grew from 46 per cent in 1955, to 51 per cent in 1965, 55 per cent in 1975, 61 per cent in 1985 and 67 per cent in 1995.[3] However, their participation was, overwhelmingly, unlike men's. Not only was there strong segregation, with men and women working in different occupations and in different industries, but women were also much more likely to be working part-time. Their earnings were providing a vital supplement to the 'family' wage, which was in most cases becoming insufficient to provide a whole household with all the goods and services that were newly becoming 'essential' in an increasingly materialistic post-war consumer society (indeed, in many occupations and industries, the male wage had always been too low to keep a family out of poverty). But their income was generally secondary. Women who lived outside a heterosexual couple struggled to find jobs that could provide a decent income.

TACKLING THE BROADER SOCIAL CAUSES OF INEQUALITY

Feminists argued that this secondary employment status could not be addressed simply by making changes within the market for paid labour. It could only be understood by looking at women's role in providing unpaid labour in the home.

The gender division of labour in the home shapes the gender division of labour outside the home in multiple ways. One of these relates to the value placed on women's skills. The skills they exercise unpaid in the home (e.g. cleaning, preparing food, and care work) tend to have a low value on the labour market (because they have low scarcity). Thus, women are not only more likely than men to be assigned such roles in the money economy, but these jobs are also likely to be paid less than those carried out by men. This has historically been associated with low levels of professionalisation, organisation and bargaining power for workers in such occupations.

A second factor relates to the time constraints placed on women with household responsibilities, both in terms of the amount of time available and its disposition. The time-tables of domestic work restrict availability on the labour market both temporally and spatially. In a process of mutual adaptation, in most developed economies, this has led to the creation of part-time, proximate jobs designed to meet the needs of women who are on a short leash from their homes. On the one hand, women seek out jobs that can be combined logistically with their reproductive responsibilities. On the other hand, employers, seeing that this offers a cheap way to fill them, design jobs so that they meet these needs.

In some cases, this mutually reinforcing process extends not just to the design of shift patterns that mesh with the daily rhythms of family life, but also to longer-term temporal rhythms created by the institutional requirements that shape social reproduction, for example offering 'term-time only' contracts to parents of school-age children. Needless to say, such jobs tend to offer low rewards and poor prospects for advancement. This means that men are more likely to fill jobs that require extended working hours or long-distance travel, jobs which are more likely to be well rewarded. It should be noted, however, that there are exceptions to these patterns. At the bottom end of the labour market, women workers may be forced to override the needs of their families in order to obtain an income. Examples of this are migrant women obliged to leave their own children behind and travel to another continent to carry out low-paid reproductive work for others, and office cleaners who have to make contingent arrangements in order to work night shifts. At the other extreme, relatively privileged women can enter the labour market on similar terms to men by paying others to carry out their reproductive work.

Other mutually reinforcing patterns have created expectations that career interruptions as a result of childbirth and caring will lead to lower achievement by women, which in turn results in different normative models of educational and occupational choice for girls. What is the point of expensively equipping a young woman with the skills for a high-flying job if she is going to give up work as soon as her first baby is on the way?

These historical patterns have shaped a reality in which women have been less, or differently, qualified than men, which in turn has led to them being steered into different, generally lower-paid, occupations. The resulting formation of a large pool of underqualified women workers has also led to male workers treating them as a threat that will undercut their hard-won wages and conditions.

In sum, these patterns, in combination, have created a situation where there is a systematic segregation of women in the paid workforce along multiple dimensions including occupation, sector, working hours, contractual status, pay and working conditions. These patterns are underpinned by a culturally embedded normative assumption that, in an ideal world, 'a woman's place is in the home'. And these norms, in turn, create sanctions that serve to reinforce the boundaries between male and female spheres, both inside and outside the paid workforce.

The long-standing, and deeply embedded, nature of these patterns does not, of course, mean that they have remained unchanged. On the contrary, new technologies and innovations in work organisation have brought many twists and turns, with each new development creating both opportunities and threats for women, but also for men. Automation, for example, simplified some labour processes, resulting in women being substituted for skilled and well-organised male workers in some industries, with the change typically accompanied by lower wages and different shift patterns. Standardisation of procedures associated with digitalisation in bureaucratic organisations resulted in women being recruited as managers at precisely the moment these managerial jobs were being deskilled and transformed. An example of this is the role of the manager of a branch of a bank or building society. In earlier periods, when such jobs were overwhelmingly filled by men, their responsibilities included deciding, as a matter of personal judgement, which customers should get a mortgage. By the time it had become usual for women to be branch managers, such decisions were made by standard algorithms and the manager's job reduced to that of a team leader. The development of call centres created new kinds of part-time work, in different locations from the face-to-face customer service jobs that they replaced. The combination of information and communications technologies that made it possible for digitisable work to be carried out remotely was seen as an opportunity to allow people (most likely to be women with domestic responsibilities) to work from home, creating a new kind of two-tier segmentation in information processing work.

Every development in the division of labour has thus brought changes, but none of these seems yet to have posed a serious challenge to the underlying patterns of gender segregation, even when introduced under a cloak of social innovation in a manner that is apparently progressive, emancipatory and unisex. The problem of women's inequality in the workforce has dramatically changed in its visible forms but remains, at root, the same. Why?

THE PROBLEM OF UNPAID DOMESTIC LABOUR

For second-wave feminists, the household division of labour was the fundamental obstacle to true equality between women and men. How was it to be overcome? In the intensive debates of the 1970s several different ideas were put forward, some resurrected from earlier feminist debates at the beginning of the twentieth century.

One important demand was for the socialisation of the labour involved in housework and family care. It was argued that, instead of having these activities carried out in isolation in labour-intensive ways by individual women, each in a separate household, it would be both more equitable and more efficient to have them provided collectively – for example in public laundries, nurseries, and local canteens. Such demands had inspired some of the innovations of the Attleean welfare state in creating new health and social services, and they underpinned a wave of feminist political activism in support of expanding public services (and, later, in defending them against cuts in welfare spending). As the twentieth century progressed, the welfare state provided a range of services, from mother-and-baby clinics to meals-on-wheels, from nurseries to day centres for the elderly. But as time went by, more and more political energy went into defending existing services against cuts rather than campaigning for new ones, and the original impetus to demand new public services to substitute for unpaid housework faded.

A second approach was to demand payment for housework. The nearest thing to this in the mid-twentieth-century British welfare state was child benefit – a universal benefit paid to all households for each child and, significantly, generally paid to the mother. This was nowhere near high enough to cover the whole cost of raising a child, but it did make a significant contribution to household budgets. It was supplemented by other means-tested benefits, paid to single parents, people with disabilities, their carers, and the unemployed. This demand has evolved in some quarters into campaigns for a universal basic income (UBI), discussed in chapter 6. Despite a growing public debate about UBI, actual progress on this front has gone into reverse, with restrictions on entitlements to benefits, and cuts in the value of benefits, leading to a major growth in poverty, including child poverty.

A third approach to the 'housework problem' looked to technology for salvation. Labour-saving devices, it was thought, would dramatically reduce the time required for housework, as well as the skills needed to do it, leading to men taking on a much greater share of household labour. While it is certainly true that huge advances have been made in the development of technologies for use in the household (think of Alexa, or smart fridges) they do not necessarily reduce the amount of labour time devoted to housework, often just substituting one kind of work for another.

THE MARKETISATION AND COMMODIFICATION OF HOUSEWORK

Less anticipated was what actually seems to have happened in practice – a huge growth in the purchase of household services in the market, substituting buying for making.

Research shows that the gender gap between women and men in terms of daily minutes spent on 'core housework' (defined as cleaning, cooking and clothes care) has indeed been shrinking. In 1961, women in the UK did 195 more minutes of this type of housework per day than men; by 2005 this gender gap had been reduced to 74 minutes. However, this was not so much because men were doing more housework – their daily minutes rose only from 24 to 48 during this period – but because women were doing less – down from 219 to 122. Women still do significantly more housework than men, with a ratio of 1.85 in the UK.[4]

Adding care work into the story reinforces this picture of gender inequality. According to a 2018 ILO study, UK women do a total of 232 minutes care work per day (compared with 131 for men), of which 32 (15 for men) are classified as 'domestic services for their own final use within the household', and 200 (116 for men) as 'caregiving services to household members'.[5] Men do more hours of paid work than women and it is sometimes pointed out that if you add up the number of paid and unpaid hours of work done by men and by women the totals are quite similar. However, as Jonathan Gershuny points out, 'This is not equality, since men do substantially more paid work, and women do substantially more unpaid. And this inequality has, in turn, important consequences for inequality in earnings.'[6]

What seems to have been happening is that households, with all adults increasingly obliged to go out to work, are turning to the market to buy services instead of producing them themselves. Paying other people to do your housework is not a new phenomenon. Before the Second

World War very many people were employed as live-in domestic servants in the UK, and significant numbers continued after the war to work as cleaners, childminders, nannies, gardeners and 'helps'. During the heyday of the twentieth-century welfare state it was, however, rare for working-class households to pay for household services other than, perhaps, occasional provisions like window-cleaning, dressmaking or carpentry. There was, nevertheless, an increasing trend to substitute buying for making or mending – for example purchasing ready meals from the supermarket instead of cooking a meal from scratch, or buying a new pair of socks rather than darning old ones.

Recent years have seen a sharp acceleration in the marketisation of domestic labour. Several factors have converged to compress the time available for housework. These include the growing labour force participation of women, demographic changes leading to an increase in the need for elder care, the increasing intensity of work, and an accelerating tendency for work obligations to spread beyond the confines of the formal working day, with workers expected to be on call or to check for emails or text messages from employers or clients outside normal working hours. The trend towards project-based working and management by results also leads to a culture in which workers put in unpaid overtime in order to meet deadlines or fulfil performance targets. Added to this is the growing tendency, discussed in the preceding chapter, for people to take on extra work on top of their main job – a trend that is largely driven by low wages and poverty.

Public spending cuts have drastically reduced many services previously provided by the state. For example, closures of day centres, youth centres and playgroups, or the withdrawal of meals-on-wheels and home help services, force families to draw on their own time and resources to provide substitutes. Together, these have put intense time pressure on household members, making it difficult if not impossible for them to spend quality time together and communicate in a relaxed way, and intensifying squabbles about who does what.

This time squeeze has in turn led to a growth in demand for paid help with household chores. Because much of the work involved in providing household help such as cleaning or babysitting is carried out in the informal economy, paid in cash, it is difficult to find reliable statistics on the precise scale of this growth. Popular conceptions of domestic work associate it with underdeveloped economies and see it as part of a trend that is historically declining. However, there is evidence that, far from declining, it is actually growing – and growing fast. For example, one UK survey found that in 2011 (when the economy had not yet recovered from the 2008 financial crisis) approximately 6 million people in the UK were employing a cleaner, compared with 5 million a decade earlier.[7] A third said that they did so because they did not have the time to do the work themselves, a proportion that rose to nearly half among those aged 18 to 32. Another survey, using a broader definition that included window-cleaners, gardeners and handymen, found that one UK household in three was paying for some form of domestic help in 2016, with particularly high rates among the under-35s. Even among households with incomes of less than £20,000 per year, one in four were doing so.[8] To these services involved in maintaining the home can be added other kinds of privately procured paid domestic work such as babysitting and care for the elderly.

ONLINE PLATFORMS AND THE HOUSEHOLD TIME SQUEEZE

In the past, the people who could provide these services might have been found through personal recommendations, leaflets through the letterbox, advertisements in the local newsagent's window or the Yellow Pages. Nowadays, they are increasingly acquired through online platforms. Whether you need a cleaner, a babysitter, a handyman, a dog-walker or a gardener you are likely to start with a Google search, while an app on your phone is the simplest way to organise the delivery of a ready meal when you are too exhausted to cook, or a car to take you to a hospital appointment because the bus service has been axed.

Research I carried out with colleagues at the University of Hertfordshire provided dramatic evidence of the scale of platform use. In 2019, six out of ten (60.7 per cent) UK adults said that they had been users of platform services – the equivalent of 29.7 million people across the UK. This proportion was somewhat higher among people with more money to spare – around three quarters of those earning more than £35,000 a year and around two-thirds of those earning more than £20,000 a year said they use these services – but it was also widespread among poorer groups, with over half (50.9 per cent) of people earning less than £20,000 saying they used platform services. Platform users were more likely to be working full-time and less likely to say that they were full-time homemakers, pointing to the importance of the time squeeze in this context.[9]

It would be wrong, then, to see users of platform services as a privileged bourgeoisie being served by a new precarious servant class. The platform economy is, rather, a marketised exchange of services among households, many of which are poor households. Strikingly, people who do platform work are themselves very likely also to be customers for these services. Looking specifically at services provided in the household (including cleaning, babysitting, gardening, plumbing, repair of appliances, electrical work, carpentry and personal services such as hairdressing, manicure or massage), we found no less than 94.5 per cent of those who said that they work via a platform providing these services at least weekly were also customers for them. Trend data shows a very rapid growth, with the proportion of the UK population purchasing such platform services at least once a year rising from 23.8 per cent in 2016 to 31.4 per cent in 2019, and the proportion providing the labour to supply them at least weekly doubling from 2.7 per cent to 5.4 per cent over the same three-year period.[10]

Platform work seems to form part of a rapidly growing and self-reinforcing trend – a vicious cycle wherein the need for extra income leads to working longer hours, leaving less time available for housework, leading to greater use of platforms which, in turn, increases precarious work still further, as shown in the accompanying diagram.

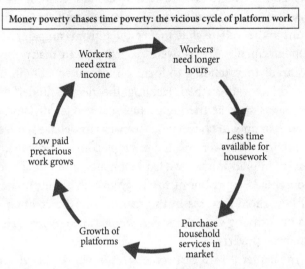

Money poverty chases time poverty: the vicious cycle of platform work

Workers need extra income → Workers need longer hours → Less time available for housework → Purchase household services in market → Growth of platforms → Low paid precarious work grows

Because women still do disproportionately more household work than men, they are also more affected by the grinding stress of being caught up in this cycle. This has knock-on effects not just on their work-life balance but also on their ability to participate on equal terms in the labour market. If inequalities in the domestic division of labour between men and women cannot be resolved, then there is little hope of achieving genuine social and economic equality outside the home.

CONCLUSIONS

This chapter has looked at how the twentieth-century welfare state was founded on the basis of a profoundly unequal model of gender relations, with the presumption that a 'normal' household consisted of a male breadwinner and a female housewife and mother. It went on to discuss how this model was challenged, and the adaptations to the welfare state that resulted from campaigns for gender equality. These were partial and, in many ways, contradictory, tending to focus on formal equality in the workplace rather than tackling the deeper underlying problems such as the highly unequal gender division of labour in unpaid housework. Cutbacks to welfare services, combined with women's increasingly compulsory participation in paid work, have led to a major time squeeze on households, contributing to a large growth in the purchase of household services in the market and the creation of an intensifying vicious cycle in which time poverty drives financial poverty.

In chapter 8 I suggest some ways in which this vicious cycle could be broken, and platform technologies used to increase the supply of household services, improve the quality of employment, and contribute to the development of a welfare state which genuinely promotes equality between men and women.

CHAPTER FIVE

Recalibrating the Mechanisms of Redistribution

The previous chapters have shown that the welfare state we have today is very far from meeting the ambitious aims laid out for it in the mid twentieth century. Instead of redistributing from the rich to the poor it does the opposite. Instead of giving workers a basic set of rights that protect them from exploitation it bolsters the power of unscrupulous employers. Instead of promoting equality between men and women it reinforces patterns that perpetuate these inequalities. Instead of providing a safety net that protects the vulnerable from penury, hunger, pain and homelessness it has increased the numbers sleeping rough, dependent on food banks and deprived of benefits. Rights to benefits, housing and employment protection are increasingly not universal but contingent. They are things that have to be begged for, hedged around with complex legal and bureaucratic rules, involving time-consuming and humiliating form-filling, means tests and other demeaning checks, administered increasingly by poorly qualified staff employed by outsourced companies driven by the imperative to meet targets rather than any humane assessment of actual need. Meanwhile many publicly owned national assets have been handed over to corporations to milk for profit.

INVERSION OF BEVERIDGE'S ORIGINAL AIMS

The British welfare state is increasingly taking on the character of a vast workhouse, but one in which, unlike its nineteenth-century predecessors, there is not even a roof to keep out the weather. You cannot turn on the radio, glance at a newspaper or log on to social media without being inundated with evidence of the sickening impact of this on the daily lives of citizens: the growing numbers sleeping on the streets; the exponential increase in the numbers of people using food banks; the 'sanctioning' of claimants for such trivial offences as arriving a few minutes late for an appointment at a Job Centre; people declared 'fit for work' when they are on their deathbeds; the crisis in social care. A cursory Google search will throw up so many horror stories that many decent people now find themselves in an almost catatonic state, beyond shock, struggling for words, let alone ideas that might inform an adequate response.

Suffice it to say that the welfare state these decent people grew up taking for granted (far from perfect as many knew it to be) has morphed into a regime that has anything but welfare as its prime objective. Increasingly run by multinational corporations with a firm eye on the bottom line, via incompetently drafted service contracts whose main feature is a requirement to meet targets, the main effect of this regime is to harass and humiliate the most vulnerable people in society and transform them into a forced reserve army of labour, with no sense of entitlement, coerced to work below the cost of subsistence.

THE IDEOLOGICAL UNDERPINNING

This regime is kept in place not just by the force of law but also ideologically, by a series of unexamined shibboleths perpetuated in a variety of ways – by the mass media, political parties and others – that are increasingly taken for granted by the general public. These beliefs have permeated popular understanding so thoroughly that it requires considerable effort even to question them, or to convince others that they are not common sense.

One common misconception is the notion that the British welfare state is too generous and that this is why so many immigrants are attracted to the UK. Linked to this is the idea that the welfare bill is too high and that the only way the economy can claw its way out of recession and into growth is by further cuts to services and benefits. Perniciously associated with this is the belief that there are too many benefit scroungers stealing from hard-working people, scroungers who need to be flushed out and punished.

A further set of mistaken assumptions hampers the public understanding of redistribution, the tax system and the economy: that tax credits are a progressive innovation; that raising the minimum wage would place an intolerable burden on small businesses and make life impossible for the entrepreneurs who create jobs; that increasing income tax punishes hard-working people; that raising corporation tax drives out investment and destroys jobs; and that the private sector can deliver services more efficiently than the state. Cumulatively, these misconceptions lead to the conclusion that there is no alternative to continuing the neoliberal policies of the last 40 years, further hollowing out the welfare state and legitimising austerity.

Any attempt to rebuild the welfare state in a way that remains true to its original spirit will have to look deeper than the particular forms that current institutions take and uncover the principles on which they were founded: the principles of redistribution and universality without which the goals of fairness, equality and freedom from Beveridge's 'giant evils' cannot be met. In the rest of this chapter I look at the basis of certain current ideological myths to show how they undermine these principles of universality and redistribution. I do so in the conviction that understanding these processes will help us answer the questions of what sort of welfare state is desirable or achievable in these times. What alternative is there to the workhouse without walls?

A WELFARE STATE THAT FAILS TO PROVIDE WELFARE IS DYSFUNCTIONAL FOR CAPITALISM

It is often thought, on the radical left, that demands for new welfare models are necessarily 'transitional' (in Trotsky's sense): demands that cannot be met without a revolutionary change to the whole capitalist system. This may well be the case for some options, but not for those I will be discussing later in this book. I emphasise now that these demands are not necessarily revolutionary, because many of the features of the current system are actually dysfunctional for capitalism itself. This can be illustrated by just a few examples.

Here's one: in the accelerating speed of innovation in competitive global labour markets, capitalist enterprises have an insatiable appetite for creative workers who can come up with a stream of ideas for new products, new processes and new ways of applying these in new markets. Such companies can therefore only benefit from state-provided education systems that encourage creative thinking. Capitalist enterprises also benefit from welfare systems that provide an income sufficient to enable people to set up innovative new businesses which, if they succeed, they can then take over or copy (look at the fashion and music industries). Capitalism therefore benefits directly from well-funded public education and generous benefit systems, as the thriving economies of the Nordic countries demonstrate very well.

To take another, smaller and specifically UK example: employers are now finding it so difficult to recruit workers with children because of the lack of affordable childcare that in 2014 the Confederation of British Industry began campaigning for an expansion of free childcare. Again, there is a recognition that employers benefit directly from generous state services.[1]

Capitalism has historically profited greatly from the NHS and from the strong welfare states to be found in the Nordic countries. It is much easier for companies to locate in places where they know, for example, that the workforce will have its health taken care of by the state, thereby avoiding the need to negotiate expensive private health insurance schemes (as many large US-based companies had to do in the latter part of the twentieth century). Although capitalism is endlessly inventive in its ability to profit even from poverty, too much poverty leads to a drop in consumer demand which is bad for business, and too much destitution will, sooner or later, lead to the risk of breakdowns in public health and public order. These are not good for most capitalists either.

The demands outlined in the next two chapters are, I believe, capable of being met without bringing capitalism to its knees, and, in the spirit of mid-twentieth-century social democracy, could be introduced in a way that improves the quality of life for citizens without destroying capitalism. Indeed, some might lead to new opportunities for innovation and growth. I leave it to others to formulate more revolutionary demands.

THE EXAMPLE OF TAX CREDITS

But first it is important to gain some clarity about the mistaken views that impede constructive thinking about redistribution and universality. To illustrate how complex a task it is to unravel the direct and indirect ways in which money gets redistributed and how different political interests are intertangled, I begin with the case of tax credits.

In terms of its effects, the introduction of tax credits was perhaps the most genuinely redistributive initiative taken by the New Labour government of the 1990s in that it really did boost the incomes of some of the most deprived families and improve the quality of life for poor households with children – or at least prevent it deteriorating further in the increasing polarisation of wealth that was taking place at the time. But from whom did this redistribution take place?

The Labour government was elected in 1997 with a clear mandate to do something about low wages and child poverty. British trade unions had historically been split on the issue of a statutory minimum wage, with the unions representing better-organised workers arguing that it would hinder their ability to raise wages through collective bargaining at company or sector level (ignoring the pleas from feminists, as well as representatives of low-paid and unorganised workers, who insisted that 'a floor is not a ceiling'). But in the long bitter Tory years, when Labour was in opposition and the unions saw the continuing erosion of their rights, as well as a fall in the real value of wages, they came round to the idea. At this point, the Labour government was faced with a choice: it could set a high minimum wage (which, once set, would have been very difficult to remove), or a low one – in the realisation that this would not be enough to keep households out of poverty if the adults in them were working part-time or on low wages – and then buttress this low wage with additional means-tested forms of financial support.

It chose the latter option, and in 1999 introduced a minimum wage that was low (by European standards) along with the family tax credit system. This was intended to avoid the various 'poverty traps' and 'unemployment traps' that had existed previously, whereby poor adults with children actually lost money if they came off benefit to work in low-paid or precarious jobs, so there was no incentive for them to enter the labour market. The tax credit system was, in other words, part of a stick-and-carrot scheme designed to get people into work and off benefits, and several of the benefits they would previously have been entitled to were removed in the process of introducing it.

At the time, this low minimum wage/tax credit combo was greeted by most people on the left as a sign that the government was moving in a progressive direction. An alternative view is that it was doing the very least it could get away with, desperate to find a solution that would not upset big business.

A case study of neoliberal lobbying: the Mckinsey Global Institute and the tax credit

This can be illustrated by evidence from a 2004 book called *The Power of Productivity: Wealth, Poverty and the Threat to Global Stability*, which provides a case study of the influence of neoliberal thinking on policy.[2] The author, William Lewis, has an interesting curriculum vitae. According to the blurb, he 'held several policy-making positions in the US Departments of Defense and Energy and also served in the World Bank', before going on to become a partner at McKinsey and Company and then found the McKinsey Global Institute. I first became interested in the McKinsey Global Institute in the early 2000s when I was doing research on offshore outsourcing, and it was issuing reports claiming that this practice was not only good for globalisation in general and the US economy in particular but also good for American workers (because it helped bring down the cost of consumer goods and also helped US businesses thrive). As I read the Institute's reports, I realised that it had a finger in a lot of other pies too.

Lewis is nothing if not a name-dropper, and in the book he describes how, shortly after the Labour government was elected in 1997, 'Gordon Brown, the new chancellor of the exchequer, contacted me through Adair Turner, a former partner of mine who was then head of the Confederation of British Industries ... He said that during the UK election, our study of France and Germany was the best economic analysis he had read ... and offered to pay something for a UK study.'[3]

The book goes on to address a range of issues that at first seem quite disparate: the cost of land in various countries and the ease with which it is possible to get planning permission to change its use; productivity in various industries, including a curiously detailed comparison of a small shop in a favela in Brazil with a supermarket; and ... family tax credits! The connection between these diverse issues was not immediately obvious and it took me a while before things clicked into place. The key question to ask was where the Institute got its money from, and the answer made the connection clear: its three biggest contributors were Walmart, Tesco and Carrefour, the three biggest retailers in the world at the time.

Each of the policies Lewis advocated so strenuously (and for which he had gained the ear of political leaders in many developing countries – including India – as well as the leading G7 economies) was a policy that directly benefited the global supermarket chains that were his paymasters. In the 2000s, Walmart stood to benefit more than almost any other US company from offshore outsourcing to China. Offshoring made it possible to bring in shiploads of cheap consumer goods from China and sell them by the million to poor US families for whom the rock-bottom prices of these products concealed the real fall in the value of their incomes. Meanwhile the deindustrialisation of large swathes of America added to the numbers of desperate people prepared to work for the company for equally rock-bottom wages. Interestingly, opinion poll after opinion poll has shown that most US workers would prefer to forego some of the cheapness of goods in favour of decent jobs with decent wages.[4] But workers are always an electoral minority and, under both the Clinton and Bush governments, it was a safe bet that the larger electorate (including the elderly and the economically inactive as well as workers) would be more likely to vote for those who could deliver cheap goods rather than fair wages. This situation changed little under Obama and Trump.

What about the obsession with planning laws? Lewis rants at some length about how difficult it is to get planning permission for new developments in many parts of the world, and complains bitterly that Europeans tend to over-value their historic buildings. Why does this annoy him so much? Because planning restrictions make it difficult for Carrefour and Tesco to build huge out-of-town hypermarkets.

What about small firms in developing countries? The slum traders in Brazil, it seems, are inefficient. According to Lewis, retail productivity would be much higher if everybody shopped in a supermarket. He concedes that the favela shop his team observed was providing employment for the woman who ran it, and that she could take care of her child while she worked there, but maintains that she would be much better off working in a supermarket where, 'if the child were the problem, she could work part time'.[5] He presents the informal economy as being in unfair competition to the big supermarket chains because small traders are not paying tax.

And what about family tax credits? Lewis argues that, along with restrictive planning laws, a high minimum wage is one of the 'main enemies of economic growth',[6] holding back European productivity more than any other factor. It is repeatedly asserted that the Earned Income Tax Credit is a better way of achieving after-tax income distribution objectives than the high minimum wage[7] – the mantra that had such a receptive hearing from New Labour. Seen from the point of view of companies like Carrefour, Tesco and Walmart, the advantages are obvious: it enables them to pay low wages in the knowledge that these will be topped up by a direct subsidy from the state.

On the face of it, tax credits really do seem to solve many problems: they lift (some) people out of extreme poverty; they remove some of the 'traps' that previously made it difficult for people to move off benefits and into work without being financially worse off; and they can be claimed by people without a previous record of paying contributions into the national insurance system.

It takes deeper investigation to understand that while they may seem on the face of it to be a subsidy from richer taxpayers to the poorest and neediest in our society, they are mainly a subsidy from the taxpayer to employers. Viewed in this way, tax credits can be seen as a crucial component of the architecture of neoliberal employment regimes, which, under a benign guise, are actually dismantling the welfare entitlements that were fought for in the twentieth century.

Tax credits in the context of income tax

Before looking at alternatives, it is useful to look at how tax credits relate to income taxes. Income taxes were first introduced in Britain in 1798 by William Pitt to pay for the Napoleonic Wars. Right from the beginning, they were graduated, starting at two pence in the pound (there were 240 pence to the pound so this was less than 1 per cent) on incomes over £60 (the equivalent of about £5,500 in today's money) and increasing to a maximum of two shillings in the pound (there were 20 shillings to the pound so this equalled 10 per cent). Those earning less than £60 a year paid no income tax. Although eroded in several respects, the principle is still the same. In 2019, the 'personal tax allowance' (the amount of earnings on which you pay no tax at all) was £12,500. On earnings from £12,501 to £50,000 the tax rate was 20 per cent, rising to 40 per cent on incomes between £50,001 and £150,000, with a maximum of 45 per cent for people earning above that level. Tax credits (which the UK government describes as 'benefits') are in the process of being transformed into 'Universal Credit' which, as I write, is still not completely rolled out. Before Universal Credit was introduced, two main types of tax credit were in operation. One was for people with children, payable to households earning less than £16,000 a year (if they had one child) or £32,200 (if they had two or more children). The other was for childless single people earning less than £13,000 a year or childless couples with a joint income of less than £18,000. Universal Credit, paid monthly in arrears, replaces six other existing means-tested benefits and sets the level of subsistence for any given household according to various standard formulae. The allowance for a single claimant under the age of 25, for example, is set at £251.77 per month; that for a couple aged over 25 is £498.89 per month. Allowances are paid after deducting any earnings, again according to complex formulae.

If the original tax credit model was flawed, that for Universal Credit is worse. One study summed it up in these words:

> Universal Credit is in crisis. Far from being an aid to people on low income, it has pushed many further into debt, use of foodbanks, rent arrears, and sometimes homelessness … Even worse than the five-week wait before it starts, Universal Credit payments fluctuate monthly, yet with a rigid assessment schedule which does not take into account actual paydays. Universal Credit therefore makes it impossible for claimants to plan payment of their bills more than one month in advance, and the draconian repayment demands for people who need Universal Credit advances leave some with nothing to live on despite their claim starting. Cuts, in the form of the two-child limit, the bedroom tax, the Local Housing Allowance, the Benefit Cap, the 'Income Floor' for the self-employed, promised new in-work conditionality, reductions in severe disability payment, and reductions in passport benefits such as free school meals and exemptions from National Health

Service charges, have squeezed the incomes of people on Universal Credit. The cuts have also led to lower take-up, leaving many to rely on family, friends, and debt, to get by.[8]

What any credit-based system effectively does, after various means tests have been applied and bureaucratic procedures followed, is top people's income up: the state adds to it, rather than subtracting from it as it does when it takes income tax. On the face of it, this seems quite sensible. So, what is so invidious about this approach? Here, it is important to look concretely at how it functions.

The practical effects of applying the credit system

People who are claiming tax benefit are working people in badly paid work. They have lost the right to refuse low-paid jobs because the conditions for obtaining unemployment benefit ('jobseeker's allowance') have been made so penal that they are 'sanctioned' if they refuse to take whatever job they are thrust into. Unable to seek work that is more fulfilling or better suited to their qualifications, they are obliged to accept what they are offered in terms of wages and conditions. And when they work for wages that are below subsistence level and claim a tax allowance, it is their employers who benefit. Tax credits are therefore a way to subsidise employers who pay below-subsistence wages. In this process, the direct link between hours worked, pay and survival is broken: if workers get a pay increase, the amount of the increase is simply knocked off the credit. This means that there is little or no incentive to join a union and campaign for better pay. Why pay union dues, money that a low-paid worker can ill afford, for no financial benefit?

There are larger political implications too. The level of tax credit is set by the government in a decision in which workers have no say and can be reduced at a stroke. Reducing wage levels in this way would be much harder. Minimum wages are embedded in contracts of employment and collective agreements and can't be taken away unilaterally. This is enormously disempowering for workers and the organisations that represent them.

Benefit claimants constructed as 'scroungers'

There are also major ideological implications. Tax credits are seen by the government as a 'benefit' and therefore make up a high proportion of what is regarded as the 'unacceptably high' benefits bill. The category 'benefits claimants' can then be elided with the category 'unemployed people' or 'scroungers'. In the popular imagination, most benefit recipients are idle, although in fact, when tax credits are included, a much higher percentage of welfare spending goes to the working poor. By 2011–12, after the financial crisis, jobseeker's allowance, paid to unemployed people, accounted for only 4 per cent of all benefit spending. The equivalent figure for tax credits was 27 per cent.[9] This discrepancy has increased since then, with a continuing fall in the number of jobseekers. It was estimated in 2018 that, 'Contrary to widespread perceptions, 1 per cent of the welfare bill goes to support the unemployed (£3 billion a year) and over 30 per cent (almost £70 billion a year) goes to support those who are in work but who are paid too little to survive.'[10] Most of these 'benefits' are therefore manifestly *not* going to the idle.

Nevertheless, the demonisation of the unemployed as undeserving scroungers continues unabated. In the mass media this can be seen every day in television programmes like *Saints and Scroungers, Benefits Britain, Benefits Street, Nick and Margaret: We all Pay your Benefits* and *Tricks of the Dole Cheats.*[11] It is also visible in government advertisements encouraging people to call anonymously to report neighbours they suspect of being benefits cheats, despite the fact that, to quote the BBC, 'only about 1 per cent of all benefits are fraudulently claimed. Indeed more money is lost through administrative error than benefit fraud.'[12]

This false dichotomy between 'hard-working taxpayers' and 'claimants' doesn't just drive wedges into communities, it also legitimises further demonisation and further welfare cuts in a continuing downward spiral. An extra ingredient in this toxic stew is the role of tax credits in stereotypical thinking about immigration. Although they are actually quite hard to claim, requiring a lot of paperwork that most migrants don't have, the fact that migrants are in principle entitled to claim tax credits not only perpetuates the myth that Britain is unusually generous to its migrant workforce but also allows anti-immigrant right-wing parties to whip up resentment which is then used to legitimate even harsher cuts.

Tax credits are just one instrument among many. They must be seen as part of a larger landscape that includes other mutually reinforcing features: low minimum wages, low corporate tax, falling revenues from income taxes and national insurance contributions in real terms,[13] accompanied by the growing importance of purchase taxes to the national exchequer.

The interactions between these instruments is complex and hard to decipher beneath the rhetoric. To take one example, Gareth Morgan explains the impact of the raise in the National Living Wage (NLW) due to take effect in 2020:

> The government has announced that it is implementing the recommendations of the Low Pay Commission and that it will be the largest ever increase in NLW. For somebody on NLW who works 35 hours a week, the increase, they say, is £930 a year.
>
> They are right, and I welcome it, but they are not telling the whole story. The whole story is a little messier ...
>
> Before celebrating their windfall, someone working 35 hours a week on the NLW might want to take a closer look at the figures.
>
> On the current rate of NLW for 2019/2020, they would have annual gross pay (over 52 weeks) of £14,942.20.
>
> From April the new annual gross pay will be £15,870.40
>
> An increase of £928.20. So far, so good.
>
> Those annual pay rates are over the personal allowance for tax and the threshold for National Insurance (NI); so tax and National Insurance has to be paid on the increase.
>
> On the 2019 annual earnings, at current rates, that will be tax of £488.44 and NI of £757.22.

On the 2020 annual earnings figures, at the same current rates, that will be tax of £674.08 and NI of £868.61.

The net take home pay in 2019 is £13,696.54 and in 2020 will be £14,327.71.

So the gross increase of £928.02 becomes a net earnings increase of £631.17, still not to be sneezed at.

The NLW, though, is there to help low-paid workers. It's not the only support that is meant to be available to them. Universal Credit is the, still new and much flawed, benefit which is also meant to help low-paid workers. Its proud boast is that you're always better off in work, because you get to keep at least some of your earnings, if they increase.

Some.

Universal Credit is a means tested benefit and the higher your income, the lower the benefit. For earnings, it lets you keep 37 per cent of any extra earnings that you have. That means the government will claw back 63 per cent of those extra earnings.

That applies to the £631.17 extra that has come from the NLW. So someone working a 35 week on NLW and claiming Universal Credit will see that £631.17 a year reduced to £233.53 in real terms because their benefit will be cut.

If they are getting Council Tax Reduction, then that will be cut as well although, as there are different rules across the country, and for every English local authority, the effect will vary from place to place but it may be substantial.

The result may be that the £930 a year, trumpeted by the government, may be nowhere near the £18 a week implied but more like £2 or £3 a week.[14]

These unintended consequences are rarely visible, with any increase presented as a victory for workers and those who have been campaigning on their behalf for a higher minimum wage. Detailed debates are subsumed under the broader view in which the neoliberal policies that drive a reverse redistribution to the rich from the poor are normalised. The recipients of the (minor) increases are presented as lucky; their losses rendered invisible.

The interaction between wages and the benefit system is by no means the only example of such public discourse obscuring the underlying shift in the direction of redistribution that has been taking place below the radar of public awareness.

THE EXAMPLE OF STUDENT FUNDING

Another example is the debate about student funding. At some point – probably during the 1980s – a seismic upheaval took place in the consensus that had existed between all political parties in the post-Second World War period that the cost of higher education should be borne by society as a whole, since society as a whole would of course benefit from the results. If graduates ended up earning more than their peers then, according to this post-war consensus, there was a perfectly simple way for the state to claim back its share of this additional wealth: through income tax. It is still puzzling how quickly this logic – which appeared self-evident to many of the baby-boomer generation – broke down. The new consensus that emerged, among many Labour Party members as well as Conservatives, was that it is unfair for the rest of society to 'carry the cost' of tertiary education. Never mind the fact that many graduates are highly unlikely ever to earn more than the average (think, for instance, of where a degree in theology, or archaeology or mediaeval history might lead you). Never mind that many of the brightest will be encouraged to leave the country altogether and seek their fortunes elsewhere to avoid paying back their loans. The new common sense holds that it is right and proper that students should spend the most productive period of their adult lives after graduation paying back the cost of their tuition fees and their living costs as students, having attended institutions that, to add insult to injury, were rapidly becoming production lines of standardised forms of learning rather than centres of genuine intellectual inquiry.

How did this come about? Whatever happened to the idea that collectively passing on knowledge and wisdom to the next generation has a general social value that may not necessarily be measured in high salaries? Might not we all benefit from intelligent discussion on radio and television, well-informed local government, compassionate public service delivery, thought-provoking poetry, joyful music and inspiring sermons at the weekend? Won't well-educated adults make better and more responsible parents? When did the notion of income tax suddenly become a dangerously subversive political no-go area?

It was as if the idea of social redistribution which is both intra-generational and intergenerational across a whole society had been declared dead. The debate narrowed to a kind of bickering about how the costs were to be redistributed over an individual's own lifetime (which carries implications of intergenerational subsidy within the family): graduate tax versus various different forms of loan, with a few means-tested subsidies for those who can prove themselves exceptionally needy.

The value of an undergraduate degree on the labour market has deteriorated in proportion to the extent to which university attendance has spread across the population (increasing from 3.4 per cent in 1950 to 8.4 per cent in 1970, 19.3 per cent in 1990, 33 per cent in 2000[15] and reaching 49 per cent in 2017[16]). Many graduates end up doing low-paid menial jobs, often bearing little relation to their qualifications. Furthermore, the loan system manifestly does not work even on its own terms. It was announced in November 2014 that three quarters of graduates will never be able to pay off their debt.[17] To those who can't pay must be added those who won't. Loan repayments can, for instance, be avoided by the simple expedient of moving abroad. Students (and their parents) are in effect being asked to pay in advance for something that might never happen (enriching the financial services industry in the process, as loans are repackaged for sale on financial markets[18]). The logic that those who earn more should pay more has been stood on its head.

If the 'problem' is that graduates end up earning more than other workers, then the solution to that problem seems glaringly obvious: if and when they start doing so, let them pay it back in the form of income tax. Such a solution – tried and tested as it was in most developed countries in the latter part of the twentieth century, and still working in some – is undoubtedly simpler to run and more efficient in achieving the stated objectives of the policy that gave us the disastrous student loans. Whatever happened to the earlier common sense that income tax was the obvious way for society to recoup the extra value of higher education from those lucky enough to have received it?

Perhaps part of the rejection of this view has a psychological basis, rooted in the reality that, to some extent (albeit diminishing for many), students really *are* privileged, and always have been. This is not necessarily a financial privilege. Indeed it can plausibly be argued that a combination of the downgrading of the value of an undergraduate degree in the labour market, combined with deteriorating job prospects and the burden of paying back a student loan, will lead to the value of many degrees being financially *negative* over the course of a graduate's life. Nevertheless it can be argued that students (or at least those who do not have to combine studying with paid employment) are privileged in having a period of three or more years in their lives when they have the leisure to read and reflect and develop ideas, the opportunity to meet and get to know a variety of people from different backgrounds, to follow a thought to its conclusion, to experiment socially and sexually, to experience the satisfaction of seeing their creative effort fulfilled, and to enjoy relatively unstructured time that permits them to sit up till four in the morning talking about the meaning of life. Though it still has some traction, this is an idealised view, largely based on how student life was back in the days when students received local authority grants and did not have to pay tuition fees, and many today never achieve a fraction of these things. We know that students are increasingly likely to suffer from depression and anxiety (with an alarming increase in the suicide rate),[19] and that the pressure to earn whilst studying is constantly growing. Yet there may be just enough truth in this idealised image to rouse some resentment in those – still a statistical majority – who do not go to university, or at least to allow politicians to whip up such resentment.

Saddling students with a choice between crippling debt or emigration does not, however, seem like any kind of a solution. Wouldn't it be better to ask that students' privilege is repaid to the rest of society through putting the knowledge and wisdom that they have acquired to good use? How about requiring all students without their own caring obligations to put in a few days a year voluntary work: acting as handymen/women or gardeners to elderly and disabled people, cheering up residents in care homes, helping organise holiday playschemes for children, redecorating dilapidated community centres or whatever? Or, for those lacking social skills or not to be trusted around the vulnerable, manual work improving the environment? Both they and the rest of society would benefit far more from this kind of social redistribution of knowledge and time than by channelling their debt (and that of their parents) through the dubious conduits of the banking system. The present system does not provide a space in which such questions can even be raised, let alone properly debated. Yet it constitutes another way in which resources are stealthily redistributed from the poor to the rich.

TAX INCOME OR TAX CONSUMPTION?

Student loans are only one example of the taboo against raising income tax. More broadly, there seems to be an unshakeable conviction shared by all the major political parties that the surest way to lose an election is to suggest in your manifesto that you might want to follow such a strategy. Perhaps this is based on sound research, and most British people really do believe that paying more income tax is the worst thing that could happen to them financially. But if they do believe this, we should ask why they do so, because it flies in the face of just about all the evidence.

The belief seems to be rooted in the idea that there is some terrible unfairness involved in taking a slice from the incomes of hard-working individuals and spending it on general social goods and services. But this kind of logic is rarely applied to other taxes.

Take Value Added Tax (VAT) for example. This was introduced in the UK in 1973, as a condition of joining the European Common Market. What it replaced was purchase tax, which was levied on selected goods, at the point of production, from companies, although of course the costs were passed on to consumers. With a few exemptions, VAT is applied to all sales and purchases of goods along the value chain, with companies able to claim back the VAT they have spent on purchases and set this amount against what they have charged to customers. The tax is therefore funnelled inexorably towards the final consumer, who cannot set anything against it and must therefore pay the full whack.

As the excellent work of Richard Murphy has shown, unlike income tax, VAT is strongly regressive. In 2010, before the VAT rate went up from 17.5 per cent to 20 per cent, he compared direct taxes (income tax) with indirect ones (VAT) and concluded that:

> Direct taxes ... rise steadily as a proportion of income as incomes rise and both VAT and all indirect taxes combined do the exact opposite, falling as a proportion of income as income rises. So marked is the trend that the overall progressive effect of income tax is not enough to counter the fact that the poorest households suffer such a high rate of overall indirect tax that they end up with the highest average tax rates in the economy as a whole. The message ... is unambiguous: the poorest 20 per cent of households in the UK have both the highest overall tax burden of any quintile and the highest VAT burden. That VAT burden at 12.1 per cent of their income is more than double that paid by the top quintile, where the VAT burden is 5.9 per cent of income.[20]

A decade later, with VAT at 20 per cent, this inequality between the poorest fifth of the population and the richest fifth has worsened. Yet we find very little in the public discourse decrying this unfairness. It is overwhelmingly the redistribution of income tax that is denounced, implicitly or explicitly, generally in the form of a rhetorical question on the lines of 'Why should the hard-working taxpayer subsidise ____?' There are many ways the blank can be filled in: single parents, gender dysphoria clinics, child benefit, winter fuel allowance, bus passes, cosmetic surgery on the NHS, education for prisoners ... you name it. But I cannot recall ever hearing a sentence starting 'Why should the consumer subsidise ____?'

Talk like this both obfuscates and distorts reality. Take the example of benefits paid to parents of young children. The rhetoric implies that having children is a selfish pleasure that should only be indulged in by those who can afford it, and that those who are usually described as having 'chosen to remain childless' are unfairly penalised if a portion of their taxes is diverted in the direction of feckless parents. This ignores the larger reality that what parents are actually doing (with very little support from the state) is bringing up the next generation of workers (and taxpayers) whose labour will support their elders in their old age. Parents are thus providing what should be regarded as a public service which it makes pragmatic instrumental sense for everyone to invest in.

As with child benefit and student grants, so it is with many other forms of social redistribution. Not only do they provide efficient solutions to managing the nurture and education of the next generation and the maintenance of the social fabric; they also enrich the commons and provide the foundations of a civilised culture.

THE IMPORTANCE OF THE MINIMUM WAGE

Alongside the general prejudice against raising income tax there are other beliefs that work against redistribution.

One of these is the widespread conviction, nurtured and spread by employers and the media that do their bidding, that raising the minimum wage would damage the economy. Here, useful work has been done by the Living Wage Foundation, the trade union movement, academic researchers and others to counter this view and promote the idea of a living wage, which has now been adopted by the Labour Party, the Green Party, Plaid Cymru and the Scottish Nationalist Party as a policy goal. Even the Conservative government, after appropriating the term 'living wage' from campaigners and renaming the national minimum wage the 'national living wage', decided to increase it in 2020.[21]

Nevertheless, proponents of a high minimum wage are up against convictions that have put down deep roots. One of the most common arguments from business lobbies is that raising the minimum wage will 'destroy jobs'. Employers, they say, will simply not be able to afford the higher wages and, depending on their size and strength, will at best stop recruiting and at worst start firing people. Before the introduction of the minimum wage in 1998 the media were flooded with dire warnings along these lines. In the event, no such impacts were detected.

A very thorough survey of existing studies concluded that 'with sixty-four studies containing approximately fifteen hundred estimates, we have reason to believe that if there is some adverse employment effect from minimum wage rises, it must be of a small and policy-irrelevant magnitude'.[22] In other words, the research shows that introducing a minimum wage has no discernible effect on employment. So, arguments like these from the employers can be largely discounted. But what about other objections to the idea of a statutory minimum wage coming from other quarters? Two of these deserve special attention.

The first is that a statutory minimum wage is *incompatible with free collective bargaining*. In the past, this argument was typically put forward by trade unions representing workers in well-organised sectors who were able to bargain successfully for above-average wages and, in the process, build strong, class-conscious organisations that could (and sometimes did) use their collective muscle to campaign for broader social benefits for the working class as a whole. It was such voices, above all, that prevented the national minimum wage being placed on the Labour Party's wish-list until the 1990s, despite some weaker dissenting views from trade unions representing low-paid workers, women and freelancers.

Such views still prevail in European countries where trade unions remain strong and the coverage of collective agreements is broad. Denmark, Finland, Italy and Sweden, for example, only have minimum wage rates set through sectoral collective agreements, while Austria has a similar system but sets a low minimum wage in sectors where no collective agreements exist. Given that it is usually possible for trade unions to negotiate a wage that is higher than any statutory minimum, it is not always easy to tell to what extent such arguments are driven by instrumental factors – the belief that the only reason people join unions is to get pay increases, and a fear that members will become apathetic if they see this role being carried out by non-union organisations.

In any case, such objections are declining in importance. This is partly, perhaps, a reflection of the dwindling influence of unions in economies dominated by multinational corporations that can use the existence of a global reserve army of labour to bring downward pressure to bear on wages and conditions, and of the industrial restructuring that has shrunk manufacturing employment in the West. But it is also a reflection of the growing importance of non-wage issues in the collective bargaining agenda. Across all industries, unions are taking up issues like job security, health and safety, equality, pensions, protection against casualisation and outsourcing, and these are often the reasons people join a union rather than simply for the possibility of securing a wage increase. In the public sector, unions are under growing pressure from their members to campaign against privatisation and austerity. In the creative industries, there are burning concerns about the use of unpaid internships, ownership of intellectual property, 'fake news' and the safety of journalists. With all these other things to worry about, having a guarantee of at least a minimum level of pay might become something of a relief. For trade unions, a minimum wage is a floor below which wages cannot fall. Of course, this does not mean there is no longer a need to make sure wages rise in real terms in line with increases in the cost of living.

There are other strong arguments for raising the minimum wage that receive rather less attention. Importantly, it can contribute positively to gender equality. A high minimum wage narrows the differentials between the pay of workers near the bottom of the income scale, ironing out many gender differences in the process. It can also help to reduce other forms of discrimination and seg-regation in the labour market, for example by enabling vulnerable groups (such as people with learning impair-ments) to be integrated into the labour market without being treated as second-class workers, and ensuring that migrants who may not yet have been granted full citizen-ship are not exploited or used to undercut other workers.

Even more crucial is the redistributive effect. A high minimum wage could, at a stroke, lift large numbers of workers above the thresholds for Universal Credit or other benefits, thus substantially reducing the government's bill for providing these benefits while increasing its revenue from income tax and national insurance. Quite apart from its advantages in freeing these workers from the demean-ing grip of the benefit system, it would release funds to enable the state to be much more generous in relation to other welfare policies.

Alongside this, a high minimum wage offers a tool for obliging multinational corporations to contribute to the economies in which they operate. Even if they manage to avoid paying their fair share of taxes, if they pay higher wages then at least a bit more of their profits 'sticks' in local economies via the wage packets of those who work for them. The higher the minimum wage, the more of this money stays in the places where the value was created, and the greater the multiplier effect on local economies.

CONCLUSIONS

This chapter has focused on the mechanisms of redistri-bution underlying the shift that has taken place over the past half century in terms of who benefits and who loses financially from the welfare state. It has described how these mechanisms have been concealed under the cloak of a discourse that presents an alternative common sense that has little empirical support. It has also discussed how the combination of tax credits and low wages constitutes a huge and invisible subsidy to employers who pay low wages and low corporation tax. In drawing attention to these unspoken realities, it points to the importance of developing alternative narratives, and building new strategies based on a reversal of these negative redistribution patterns. Some of these are discussed in the next two chapters.

CHAPTER SIX

A Universal Basic Income that is Genuinely Redistributive

In the last chapter, I pointed to the importance of the principle of redistribution from the 'haves' to the 'have nots' as a necessary underpinning of any welfare state worthy of the name. The mid-twentieth-century model certainly aimed at redistribution and achieved it to some extent. However, it was also based on another important principle, that of universality. As earlier chapters have shown, the breakdown of universal entitlements to universal benefits, hedging them round with a range of conditions, bureaucratic rules, and means tests, was a feature of the erosion of this welfare model. Universal entitlements are not only much cheaper to administer but are also conducive to the development of solidarities among the recipients. Few things are more likely to provoke resentment and divisions within communities than perceptions that others are getting more than oneself. Even when resources are scarce (such as access to public housing, or non-urgent surgery) people are much more likely to accept their place in the queue if they understand that everybody is treated the same and the rules are fair.

A central challenge in designing a new welfare model is finding a balance between universality and redistribution. This is illustrated particularly clearly in the debates about the introduction of a universal basic income (UBI), a demand that has been gaining support in recent years. Until recently, the idea of a basic income, granted unconditionally to every citizen, from cradle to grave, seemed utopian. How on earth could it be paid for? Wouldn't everyone just stop working? Where would we be then?

UBI AS A FEMINIST DEMAND

I personally first came across the idea of a universal basic income in the optimistic late 1960s, in a form that later materialised in the so-called 'fifth demand' of the Women's Liberation Movement that called for 'financial and legal independence' for all women. The feminist logic underpinning this demand is powerful: not only is it degrading for anyone to have to beg or manipulate someone else for their means of subsistence, and materially damaging to that person if the money is not forthcoming; it also destroys the quality of human relationships if they are embedded in dependency. Unequal power relations like those between a husband and a dependent wife, parents and dependent teenagers or able-bodied providers and their disabled dependents can lead to a festering mess of guilt, gratitude and unexpressed anger. The results can range from dishonesty and depression to emotional and physical abuse. Economic dependence can result in 'breadwinners' feeling trapped in their roles and resentful of their dependents' apparent freedom from the constraints of the employer's clock, as well as leaving these dependents struggling with feelings of pressure to engage in coercive sex, or even put up with violence or abuse to keep a roof over their heads and those of their children.

This fifth demand, added in 1974, was accepted with widespread support across all wings of the Women's Liberation Movement. It is indeed difficult to imagine a form of feminism which does not, in a money-based society, insist that women must have their own means of financial support as a way of avoiding being trapped by economic dependence in coercive or abusive relationships.

It is therefore perhaps ironic that the question of how this financial independence should be achieved played a role in the bitter disputes within the Movement that led to the decision that the 1978 Women's Liberation Conference would be the last. Although it was by no means the only reason for the split, the espousal by many radical feminists of the demand for 'wages for housework' (developed in 1972 by the International Feminist Collective which included Selma James, Mariarosa Dalla Costa, Brigitte Galtier and Silvia Federici[1]) was for many socialist feminists the last straw. Housework, they said, should not be institutionalised as women's responsibility. It should be shared equally with men or, better, socialised, in the form of state-provided nurseries, laundries and canteens. And what would happen if women refused to do the housework for which they were paid? Would the husband, the father, or the state, taking on the role of the employer, discipline them and decide that they should not get this wage? Meanwhile radical feminists argued that reproductive work was for the benefit of all society and, since women did most of it, they should be rewarded for this. Why should they be forced into the labour market just for economic survival, when this important caring work was so socially valuable and took up so much of their time?

Nearly half a century on, some of the wounds inflicted in those debates still fester. But could it be that the demand for a UBI might be a way of healing them? Instead of posing women with the dilemma of having to choose between, on the one hand, full participation in paid work supported by public (or market) services and, on the other, an income for staying at home and taking responsibility for caring, could it, perhaps, offer them a basis for greater choice and autonomy, substituting a form of 'both/and' for a false 'either/or' dichotomy?

The contribution a UBI could make to individual independence and autonomy, and thereby to gender equality, is only one of many arguments for it. Indeed, Malcolm Torry identified over a hundred of them in his *101 Reasons for a Citizen's Income: Arguments for Giving Everyone Some Money*.[2]

UBI AND MISMATCHES BETWEEN THE LABOUR MARKET AND THE BENEFIT SYSTEM

One of these reasons is the way in which a UBI could resolve the increasingly dysfunctional interaction between the labour market and the welfare system in twenty-first-century Britain, and its associated regulatory confusion and gaps in coverage in which workers are the losers. As pointed out in chapter 2, Beveridge's national insurance model was rooted in a series of simple assumptions: that jobs were full-time and permanent, paying enough for the worker (presumed to be male) to support a dependent wife and children on the proceeds; and that circumstances that made it impossible to work, such as illness, or layoff, were temporary setbacks whose impact could be cushioned by payouts from a system into which each worker had contributed. Citizens could be classified unproblematically: employed, unemployed, self-employed, in the armed forces or a student; of working age or retired; healthy or sick; breadwinner or housewife. Despite its many imperfections, this model had enough traction to be accepted by the majority of the population as fair and sensible. Nobody wanted to go back to the dark days of the 1930s depression. Albeit with differing emphases, the welfare state was accepted pragmatically by left and right as a legitimate foundation for a democratic post-war society characterised by social harmony and economic growth.

Fast forward nearly 70 years, and these simple distinctions of the mid twentieth century have disintegrated. Women are as likely to work as men; jobs have splintered into assemblages of discrete tasks, not necessarily carried out for the same employer; training and education are spread along the life course; and the fixed boundaries of the working day and working lifetime have dissolved. As my research has shown, growing numbers of people are piecing together a patchwork livelihood from multiple sources, not knowing from one day to the next if or when they will next be paid.

For creative workers, on whose innovations an increasingly knowledge-based economy relies, the borderline between unpaid and paid work is fluid and shifting. Today's brainstorm or jam session may turn into tomorrow's multi-million-pound app or award-winning recording. Yet we still have an obsolescent benefit system that attempts to classify people neatly into those binary categories that last made sense perhaps a half a century ago: 'employed' or 'unemployed'; 'genuinely seeking work' or not.

Growing numbers of people have fallen through the cracks opened up by these incompatibilities, and they are among the most vulnerable in our society – forced to take any work that is going but often unable to claim benefit when none is available. They are caught between the rock of harsh sanctions regimes and the hard place of capricious and unreliable employers, often with no dependable source of income whatsoever. And, as we saw in earlier chapters, the numbers of these people missed by the safety net keep growing, leading to exponential rises in the use of food banks, the estimated number of rough sleepers and the number of children in poverty. In 2020, the impact of the coronavirus epidemic has been to multiply these numbers still further.

This anomalous state of affairs consumes vast amounts of the time of the officials who have to administer the system and penalises those claimants whose tangled and complex lives do not fit neatly into these categories. It also disadvantages employers who, in a competitive global economy, want to be able to access labour flexibly on demand, as well as artists and innovators who want to develop new ideas. In short, it damages not just the cohesiveness of our society but also the economy.

By avoiding the high cost of running the bureaucratic mess that is the benefit system, a UBI would thus save the state a great deal of the money currently spent on processing claims and policing benefit claimants and would eliminate the serious, sometimes life-threatening, side-effects of the Universal Credit system

Because children would be eligible for it as well as adults, it would be broadly redistributive towards households with children and thus help to alleviate the shockingly high levels of child poverty. It would also enhance inter-generational solidarity and enable family members to pool or separate their resources without changing their eligibility for caring allowances or other benefits. Because there would be no household unit of assessment it might well encourage people to live more collectively, sharing resources with friends and extended families, which could also bring environmental benefits and take some pressure off the housing market.

Further, it would make it possible for people to change their working hours flexibly and combine different jobs much more easily than at present, and would facilitate moving in and out of education or combining paid work with artistic or voluntary activities. It would also make it much easier to manage illnesses and disabilities and juggle caring responsibilities with work. Life would become smoother and simpler for freelancers or people who want to risk leaving secure employment to start a business.

With a UBI in place, the labour market could become a little less one-sided. Employers might have to offer a bit more pay to entice people into unattractive jobs, but they might also find people queuing up to fill the ones that offer high levels of personal satisfaction and reward.

At a more fundamental level, a UBI would allow people to make value judgements about what they want to do with their lives. The verdict about what is, or is not, 'work' would no longer be made by a bureaucratic authority but by the individual. If you want to live on very little and devote your life to art, music, prayer, blogging, archaeology, chasing an elusive scientific concept, conserving rare plants, or charitable work, that would be your choice. This would not just be good for individuals but spiritually enriching for society as a whole.

A UBI therefore seems to go some way towards meeting the requirements of a modern welfare state that is in line with the underlying principles of its twentieth-century predecessor. It helps to create a labour market in which workers have a degree of choice and, in times when work is not available, can access a social safety net that protects them from Beveridge's 'giant evils' without having to engage with unfair and demeaning bureaucratic rules. It promotes equality between the sexes. It rewards carers. It gives dignity and independence to the disabled and elderly. It redistributes resources towards households with children. It promotes art and culture. On the face of it, it seems to solve a huge range of problems.

THE FEASIBILITY OF UBI

These advantages are some of the reasons why this once-marginal idea is now seriously espoused in the UK by sections of the Labour Party, the Liberal Democrat Party, the Green Party, the Scottish Nationalist Party, Plaid Cymru and some trade unions. Further afield it has also been promoted (including setting up experimental schemes) in Finland, the Netherlands, India, South Africa and by high-tech entrepreneurs in Silicon Valley.

Extensive modelling work by economists and researchers like Gareth Morgan, Malcolm Torry, Howard Reed and Stewart Lansley has demonstrated that a range of options is available to a UK government for introducing such a benefit, even in what might be called a policy-neutral context, in which it is paid for by transferring funds from other benefits and abolishing the tax allowance, leaving all other features of the economy and the tax system unaltered.[3] It is, in other words, affordable. A 2019 report by Malcolm Torry goes into considerable detail showing three feasible illustrative schemes, two of which abolish the Income Tax Personal Allowance (ITPA), and one of which retains an ITPA of £4,000 p.a., offering a range of options to UK policymakers for introducing UBI at different levels, paid for by tweaking the existing tax, benefits and national insurance arrangements.[4] Each of these schemes is not only revenue neutral but also redistributes from the rich to the poor. Torry concludes that:

> this updated version of what has become a standard feasible Citizen's Basic Income scheme would be revenue neutral (that is, it could be funded from within the current income tax and benefits system); and ... the increase in Income Tax rates required would be feasible. The scheme would substantially reduce poverty and inequality; it would remove large numbers of households from a variety of means-tested benefits; it would reduce means-tested benefit claim values, and the total costs of means-tested benefits; it would provide additional employment market incentives for the large number of households no longer on means-tested benefits to the

extent that marginal deduction rates affect employment market behaviour; and it would avoid imposing significant numbers of losses at the point of implementation.[5]

In practice, of course, these models do not necessarily predict actual outcomes. Inevitably, microsimulation models like Euromod, the one used by Torry, are better able to deal with 'givens' that are clearly set out in government policy (such as tax and benefit rates) than with changes arising in the market (such as fluctuations in wage levels, prices or unemployment levels), and they cannot hope to model the full complexity of their interactions. Any government that came to power wishing to introduce a UBI would undoubtedly also want to make other changes, such as raising the minimum wage, changing the rates of income tax, creating some extra taxes, abolishing others and so on. These would radically alter the sums, as, of course, would changes in employment levels related to the dynamics of the world economy. But even leaving these points aside, it is evident that a government committed to redistribution would not find itself short of resources to redistribute.

RISKS THAT UBI COULD REDISTRIBUTE NEGATIVELY

So, what's not to like? At the headline level a UBI can seem to represent a sort of magic bullet that will solve all the problems outlined above simultaneously, and it is often promoted as such. But a closer examination of the various models proposed reveals considerable differences between them. If these differences are not recognised, attempts to operationalise it could lead at best to risks of unintended consequences and at worst to deep political fissures that could even exacerbate some of the problems UBI is intended to address.

In short, unless it is introduced carefully, a UBI could be associated with some major risks. While passing the test for universality in terms of access to benefits, it could fail the test for universal access to public services. Furthermore, in some versions it could also fail the test for economic redistribution. Indeed, it could dramatically increase the flow of resources from the poor to the rich.

Risks to public services

Let us look first at the risk to public services. By giving everyone cash, neoliberal models of UBI play along with the grain of an increasingly marketised economy in which services are individually purchased from private providers. There is therefore a risk that UBI could become a sort of glorified voucher system, undermining collectively provided public services that are designed by bodies democratically answerable to the communities they serve, under the guise of offering individual choice. Quite apart from the considerable risks that this poses to democracy, social cohesion and the quality of services (as well as the number and quality of the jobs of those providing these services), this could disadvantage individuals with special needs who require more expensive and/or specialised services than the average, exacerbating inequalities even while purporting to offer everybody the same. The provision of public services, available to all and free at the point of delivery, is an essential underpinning of any welfare state deserving of the name. It is not *necessarily* incompatible with a UBI, but care must be taken to ensure that public service provision is not unwittingly undermined by it.

This is especially important in the current UK context, where many public services have been run down and outsourced to the private sector. Even where they are not (yet) charged for, the standardisation processes that made them suitable for outsourcing have made it easy to calculate what these charges might be, and in some cases IT systems are already in place that would enable such charging to be introduced. Policymakers are faced with major challenges when they seek to improve and expand public services and bring them back under full public ownership and control. It is therefore imperative that the introduction of a UBI should be embedded with policies that protect the scope and quality of public services and their collective and universal character.

Risks to economic redistribution

Turning now to the impact of UBI on economic redistribution, one key issue is the minimum wage, discussed in the last chapter. In the abstract, the relationship between a UBI and wage levels can be argued to be either positive or negative. Some contend, quite plausibly, that a guaranteed minimum income would enable people to be much choosier about which jobs they accept, giving them options to turn down really exploitative wage rates and perhaps even providing them with a means of subsistence to strengthen their position while negotiating with employers.

Because there is rather little evidence on how UBI actually works in practice there is no way of testing hypotheses that, if the market is left to its own devices, the tendency would be for wages either to rise or to fall. A kind of common-sense logic suggests that at the very bottom of the wage spectrum, employers offering unpleasant jobs would have to raise the wages on offer because workers could no longer be forced into them out of desperation. Similarly, we can presume that trade unions representing low-paid workers would find their bargaining power with employers strengthened by the fact that UBI would offer the equivalent of strike pay in industrial disputes, enabling workers to hold out for improved offers from the employers. However, it is also possible that where jobs are more attractive, people might be prepared to do them for lower rewards.

An alternative view draws on the experience of tax credits (and now, Universal Credit), also discussed in the last chapter, to point out that providing an income top-up is, in effect, a subsidy to employers who pay below-subsistence wages. In 2015–16, this subsidy was estimated at about £30 billion.[6] Had this sum been paid out by employers as part of their wage bill then this would also have led to an increase in national insurance and tax revenues to the government. These credits therefore represent a factor which, whether inadvertently or not, increases inequalities between those who rely on wages for their livelihood and those who derive their incomes, directly or indirectly, from corporate profits.

If a UBI is not to exacerbate this state of affairs, it is imperative that it is linked to a high minimum wage, and one that can be linked to systems where workers are paid by the task, not just at hourly rates (to avoid a situation where it can be evaded by changing hourly rates of pay to piece rates). Without this safeguard there is a real danger that UBI could lead to redistribution not from the rich to the poor but from the poor to the rich.

Risks to collective bargaining

The risk of subsidising wage levels to the benefit of employers is not the only way a UBI might inadvertently work against progressive economic redistribution goals. It also risks undermining one of the few mechanisms that protects workers' economic interests: collective bargaining for employer-provided benefits. There is an established body of research showing clearly that coverage by a trade union agreement is beneficial to workers in raising wages, as well as in other ways (for example by reducing working hours and improving work-life balance). A 2017 study found that union members in Britain earn around 5 per cent more on average than equivalent non-union members.[7]

An important argument against UBI comes from social democratic parties and trade unions, especially in parts of continental Europe with a strong tradition of sector-level bargaining, who argue that its introduction would undermine their efforts to make employers pay into schemes that provide negotiated benefits, such as pensions, health insurance or childcare. A UBI provided by the state would, they contend, shift the burden of paying for it from employers to the general taxpayer. As discussed in previous chapters, general taxation is paid disproportionally by the poor, with the poorest households in the UK having both the highest overall tax burden and the highest VAT burden. UBI could therefore exacerbate inequalities, rather than reducing them, at a societal level. To avoid this risk, it is therefore also important that the introduction of UBI should be accompanied by measures that support trade unions' abilities to bargain with employers at company and sector levels, that provide protection for existing company pension schemes and other benefits, and that ensure that employers continue to contribute their share of the cost.

UBI, in other words, is redistributive only to the extent to which it is paid for by those who currently have more than their fair share of resources. If we agree that the main beneficiaries of the current, unfair system are high earners, shareholders and corporations, then the mechanisms to oblige these groups to contribute proportionally more would be a higher rate of income tax for high earners, a higher rate of corporation tax for shareholders, and a higher level of employers' national insurance contributions for employers. Without these measures, a UBI will not redistribute to the poor. It is sometimes argued that raising employers' national insurance contributions has a depressing effect on wages, but this can be simply dealt with by ensuring that the minimum wage level is set high, as already discussed.

THE PROBLEM OF ELIGIBILITY

There is yet another way in which UBI could inadvertently introduce new risks that might undermine the goal of creating a fair and equal society with opportunity for all. This is linked to the question of eligibility. If a UBI is defined as a right of citizenship, then this raises the question of entitlement: who is, or is not, a citizen? And on what basis is their right to UBI established? There is a serious danger that UBI could become linked to a narrow definition of citizenship from which some people (for example refugees, asylum seekers or residents who do not hold UK passports) are excluded. In addition to the support this might lend to racism and xenophobia, it could also lead to a two-tier labour market in which people who are not entitled to UBI become an exploited underclass. This would undercut the goal of universality.

A final condition, therefore, is that the introduction of UBI must be integrated with humane and well-thought-out policies on immigration and citizenship. This could be achieved by linking entitlement to place of residence, rather than nationality. Any definition of place of residence should be designed to ensure that people who are homeless should be included within it.

SUMMARY

It can thus be seen that UBI is not a universal panacea or magic bullet for solving the social and economic problems that face us now. Everything depends on how it is introduced and paid for. It is a realistic proposition and one that could bring huge benefits. But these benefits will accrue only if it is introduced along with other policies that buttress it. In particular, it should be regarded as part of a larger package of measures that includes strengthened and improved public services, a high minimum wage, support for collective bargaining, taxation policies that target the wealthy, and civilised and compassionate policies for the integration of refugees, asylum seekers and migrant workers.

Then, and only then, will it become a genuinely progressive initiative that can restore some dignity and security to the most vulnerable members of our society, enabling a flexible labour market to function in ways that avoid exploitation while encouraging creativity and reducing social inequality. And only then will it be genuinely compatible with social-democratic and feminist ideals, and enable us to rebuild the train-wreck that is currently all we have left of the twentieth-century welfare state that so many people worked so hard to create.

CONCLUSIONS

This chapter has examined the idea of introducing a universal basic income, concluding that, although it has many merits, including lifting people out of dependence and poverty and offering them a choice in how to live their lives, it can only be genuinely redistributive if it is introduced alongside other policies that guarantee minimum wages, protect public services, support collective bargaining and extend entitlement to all residents.

CHAPTER SEVEN

A New Deal for Labour

Chapter 3 showed some of the ways that work has been transformed over the last fifty years. Precariousness has spread as the previously dominant model of full-time permanent work has been replaced by a multiplicity of different forms of temporary, casual and on-call work. Careers have fragmented. Wages have fallen in real terms. Growing numbers of workers are only as good as their last job, having to pitch for each new promotion, job or task. There has been an exponential spread of new forms of IT-enabled management, with the direct face-to-face relationship with a line manager replaced by an impersonal, unchallengeable digital interface. Associated with this, large quantities of data on workers and their performance are being accumulated by corporations, with little or no scrutiny or accountability. The principle of universality that underpinned the twentieth-century model of employment rights has been eroded significantly and, even when rights exist in law, establishing eligibility for them has become such a confusing bureaucratic process that many are unable to claim what they are entitled to. There is clearly an urgent need for a new deal for labour.

Some of the initiatives already discussed in the two preceding chapters would serve to push things in a direction that would improve life for workers. A high minimum wage would not only raise earnings but also help to move workers out of dependence on the increasingly interlinked tax credit and benefit systems. A UBI introduced in a way that redistributes from the rich to the poor would give workers and their dependents greater security, a minimum standard of living, and protection against being bullied into accepting whatever work is available on whatever terms are offered by the employer.

Improvements in education, transport and other services also directly benefit workers. Greater investment in housing, infrastructure and sustainable energy (as proposed in the Labour Party manifesto at the 2019 general election, as well as those of the Green Party, Plaid Cymru and the Scottish Nationalist Party) would create new jobs, requiring a range of different skills and promising the possibility of developing satisfying new careers. Important though these are, it is beyond the scope of this book to discuss them. In the rest of this chapter I concentrate on those aspects of employment regulation and workers' rights that directly address the problems identified in chapter 3.

As well as the measures already discussed – expanded public services, taxation reform, welfare reform and a raised minimum wage – it seems to me that there is a need for a more fundamental rethinking of workers' rights appropriate for the new labour market conditions. In fact, a new welfare state model should put workers' rights at its very core.

A new charter of workers' rights will have to go beyond tweaking existing institutions – the benefits system, the tax system, the national insurance system, the legislation on trade union rights (although all these may also be necessary) – to establish a new legal framework that covers the entire labour market.

A CLEAR DEFINITION OF 'SELF-EMPLOYMENT'

This should start with a fundamental redefinition of what employment actually is, in recognition of the way that the mid-twentieth-century normative model has been so chipped away at that it no longer applies to large swathes of the workforce.

A good starting point is the vexed question of employment status. It is currently very difficult to determine whether or not somebody is 'genuinely self-employed', a situation exacerbated by the existence of a number of different tests and inconsistencies in the way self-employment is defined in relation to tax and social security regulations, employment regulations and how the benefit system operates. The term 'self-employed' covers a wide spectrum. At one extreme are independent entrepreneurs running their own small businesses and perhaps employing other people to work in them. Then there are freelancers – people with a distinct professional identity who provide their services (for example as journalists, designers, photographers, accountants, solicitors or IT consultants) to several different clients and negotiate their own fees for doing so. Further along the spectrum are others whose status is more ambiguous: people who work predominantly or even exclusively for the same client but are still designated 'independent contractors', 'visiting lecturers' or 'associates', and whose terms and conditions of employment are more likely to be set by the client. People who work via intermediaries, such as online platforms, typically have even less say in what work they do, how, when and where it should be done, and how it will be paid.

In the absence of a formal contract of employment, there is currently no single acid test to establish that a worker is self-employed. Drawing on a long history of case law, courts and tribunals must weigh up many different factors, such as who determines what work should be done and what should be paid for it, whether or not the worker has the right to employ someone else to do it, how continuous it is, who pays for the materials and so on, with the objective of deciding whether or not a relationship of subordination (or 'master and servant') can be said to apply. Recent test cases (involving Uber, City Sprint, Addison Lee and Pimlico Plumbers, amongst others) have ruled that workers defined by their employers as 'independent contractors' are in fact 'workers' (though not 'employees'), but it has been up to the workers and the unions supporting them to raise the money to bring these cases to court, risking their livelihoods in so doing.

The official guide to the current regulations is HMRC's Employment Status Manual,[1] but these rules are complicated and difficult to apply even in situations where all parties agree. The situation becomes a lot trickier if there is a dispute about employment status. Here, the onus is on the worker to challenge the view of the client or employer rather than the other way round. Although there have been several landmark test cases in recent years, mostly brought to the courts with the support of trade unions, this is an arduous process that puts considerable strain on the workers involved, who may be left without any source of income while the case is ongoing, leaving them without enough to live on, let alone pay for legal costs.

There is a need for new legislation that defines self-employment in such a way that the status of genuine freelancers is protected and clarified, using rules that are not only easy to understand and apply but are also consistent across the fields of taxation, employment and the benefit system. It would surely be possible to produce such a definition – after a process of consultation with trade unions, professional associations and other bodies that represent self-employed workers – one that could not only simplify the situation but also establish a larger body of rights for genuine freelancers while, in the process, distinguishing them from the pseudo self-employed, the status of 'independent contractor' and other categories of casual work that employers use in order to avoid the payment of tax and national insurance contributions and deprive workers of the rights they would have as employees.

At present, the self-employed are massively disadvantaged compared with employees. As data from the Department for Work and Pensions has reportedly shown, average earnings for those working thirty hours or more a week for themselves dropped by 30 per cent between 2008 and 2014. Fewer than one in ten self-employed people have any insurance protection against critical illness and less than a third are contributing to a pension scheme. Although it is estimated that one in ten have paid too little tax, one in four are thought to have paid too much.[2] According to a 2018 TUC report, 49 per cent of self-employed adults aged 25 and over were earning less than the minimum wage. Their average earnings in 2016–17 were £12,300 a year (a drop from £13,200 in 2015–16), compared with £21,600 for those in employment.[3]

Freelancers also face other problems. Although they are represented by trade unions in some occupations, such as journalism, acting and film production, they have relatively little voice when it comes to having their interests represented collectively. Indeed, in some cases it is argued that getting together to negotiate for minimum collective rates of pay may be regarded as forming a cartel, and fall foul of anti-competition laws. In creative industries, freelancers often face problems retaining intellectual property rights in the work that they have produced.

In short, there is a need for a new, clearly specified, set of rights and protections designed to cover only people who are genuinely freelance (working autonomously for multiple clients, able to negotiate their own rates of pay and determine how the work should be done, and free to employ assistants if need be). Clear and consistent rules should be laid down covering how these genuine freelancers should be treated by the tax and national insurance systems, and their entitlement to benefits spelled out. They should have the right to be represented by trade unions and access to schemes providing pensions and coverage for sick pay, maternity pay and other contingencies that may be brought to the surface in a full consultation process.

Once a clear legal definition of self-employment has been established, and the rights of self-employed workers specified, it then becomes possible to look at the position of those who are *not* self-employed.

CLARIFICATION OF THE RIGHTS OF DEPENDENT WORKERS AND THE OBLIGATIONS OF THOSE WHO PROVIDE THEM WITH WORK OPPORTUNITIES

Here, the starting point should be that anybody who exchanges his or her labour for money, regardless of the length of time involved, should be regarded *de facto* as a dependent worker. If there is any dispute about this status, the onus should be on the employer or intermediary by whom the worker is paid to demonstrate that this is not the case. Vulnerable workers should not have to cover the costs and risks of initiating court cases.

In the next step, a comprehensive bill of rights should be drawn up covering *all* dependent workers. This could begin by clarifying and codifying existing rights. These include rights that all workers are entitled to *as workers*, such as the right to be paid the statutory minimum wage, to receive payment for public holidays and to join a trade union without being penalised for membership.

To these should be added the statutory rights currently only available to employees. These include such things as the right to sick pay, paid holidays, maternity and paternity leave, protection against unfair dismissal, protection against discrimination and harassment, safe and healthy working conditions, and other rights set in place under law or relevant collective agreements. These rights are unproblematically available to direct employees right now (though there is sometimes in practice a difficulty in determining how regulations, such as those laid out in the Working Time Directive, apply in specific cases). They should be equally applicable, and clearly laid out, when workers are recruited or employed via intermediaries such as temporary work agencies or online platforms.

In the case of temporary work agencies there are currently rules in place that stipulate the circumstances in which the agency should take on the responsibilities of an employer and guarantee the worker the right to equal treatment with direct employees after 12 weeks in the same job with the same client. But these are hedged around with exceptions and evaded by a variety of means including employing workers through 'umbrella companies', under schemes in which individual workers are set up as separate companies with their income treated as revenues from those companies, putting them outside the scope of national insurance protection. In the case of online platforms the case law is patchy and still in development.[4] It is not even clear at present what sorts of legal entities online platforms are. They currently claim to be several different things, from technology companies to advertising agencies, seeking to absolve themselves from any responsibilities other than putting workers in touch with clients.

There is a need for clarification of these rules and a level playing field among labour market intermediaries. If a temporary work agency is responsible for paying the national insurance contributions of the workers it places with its clients, for example, shouldn't the same apply to an online platform that fulfils the same role in the labour market?

Online platforms adopt a variety of different business models and change them frequently. Some might be regarded as, in effect, offering a similar service to temporary work agencies. In other cases, their role might be closer to that of an employment agency which introduces a worker to a potential employer for a fee and then bows out of the relationship. One solution would be to classify them clearly as such agencies, bringing them automatically within the scope of existing regulations, with the onus of proof placed on the platforms if there is a dispute. Dependent workers working for platforms defined as temporary work agencies, for example, would then automatically become employees.

Consultation with trade unions, employers' associations and other bodies will be required to fine-tune any new arrangements, but the basic principle is that there should be no intervening status between that of a freelancer (clearly defined as self-employed) and a dependent worker (although there is of course no reason why a person should not engage in both types of work at different times in the same working week, month or lifetime).

The clearly specified rights of dependent workers should be reflected in equally clearly specified responsibilities of those who hire them, whether these concern accident insurance, holiday pay, sick pay or other costs normally borne by employers. If the hirer is a labour market intermediary then the default position should be that this intermediary takes on these responsibilities. If the intermediary can make a case that their role simply involves introducing the worker to a client – that they are, in effect, acting only as an employment agency – then they should be covered by the regulations governing employment agencies and the client to whom they supply the labour should carry the responsibility of the employer. A high proportion of online platforms are in effect providing services to the general public such as cleaning, babysitting or taxi services. In such cases they should be treated just like any other cleaning, babysitting or taxi company.

Clarifying the status of labour market intermediaries along with reforming the definitions of self-employment and dependent worker status are important first steps towards simplifying the situation, making the labour market more equal and making it easier for workers to feel sufficiently empowered to claim their rights, as well as developing a culture in which it is easier for them to be represented effectively by trade unions. Knowing your status and rights helps build your identity as a worker and gives you a sense of solidarity with others in the same position, perhaps tipping the delicate balance between competition and collaboration in favour of the latter.

THE NEED FOR NEW RIGHTS FOR ALL WORKERS IN THE DIGITAL AGE

The erosion of traditional forms of employment status and protection is, however, only one of many symptoms of deteriorating working conditions and the loss of workers' voice in Britain today. A profound dehumanisation of work seems to be taking place, making a mockery of the notion of 'human resources management' as a description of how the organisation of work and the management of workers is actually practised across much of the labour market. The general 'platformisation' of work has introduced a situation where a high proportion of workers (a proportion which grew exponentially during the coronavirus lockdown period in spring 2020) experience their daily interaction with their managers and team-mates not as an encounter between human beings, where problems can be addressed collectively and personal issues raised and discussed, but as an anonymous interaction with a website or an app, in which they are required to fill in online forms, parting with a good deal of personal information as they do so, in order to achieve a standard result (for example to claim money that is owing, report a problem, book leave, apply to join a new team or work on a new task, or report on the hours they have worked).

In the process, they may be 'feeding' the algorithms that are increasingly used to monitor and assess their performance with information that will enable this performance to be controlled even more tightly in the future. Qualitative aspects of their work – such as the care they put into satisfying clients, the help they give to struggling colleagues, or the excellence of their work – may go unnoticed, unless they are addressed through specific initiatives such as asking customers (who may be ignorant or prejudiced or motivated by the hope of getting a refund or price reduction) to rate their work on a score of one to five. Such forms of digital management may coexist with a range of other practices that are detrimental to health and well-being, such as the need to be available at a moment's notice to respond to demands to report for work.

I have often referred in the preceding chapters to the third quarter of the twentieth century when the ingredients of the welfare state we have inherited were put in place. The late 1960s and early 1970s were a particularly fertile period, in the UK as in other countries, for the development of legislation that codified existing good practice and created new universal rights for workers and obligations for employers. I have already referred to the wave of legislation that brought in minimal rights for equality in, for example, the Race Relations Act, the Equal Pay Act and the Sex Discrimination Act. Other important pieces of legislation during this period were the Health and Safety at Work Act of 1974 and the Employment Protection Act of 1975.

It seems to me that what is needed now is new legislation, on the same comprehensive scale and with the same universal scope as these two important Acts, putting in place a new set of rights for workers in the twenty-first century, building on these past achievements but taking into account the very different technological and organisational environment in which work is now situated. A broad consultation process would be needed to determine the scope and details of any such legislation and I would not wish to pre-empt this. So, without attempting to be comprehensive, all I will do in the rest of this chapter is discuss some of the issues that I think it should address.

To start with health and safety issues, it is clear that the definition of the 'workplace' in existing legislation needs to be updated to take account of the fact that growing numbers of workers may be working from multiple locations, including in public spaces, and that, furthermore, some of the risks to their health and safety may be taking place in cyberspace. This should be reflected in the kinds of insurance that are provided as well as the training given to workers, their managers and their union representatives. Attention should be paid to psycho-social risks, as well as physical ones, taking account of such issues as the stress resulting from the precariousness of work and the associated inability to plan ahead, as well as new risks linked to online abuse and bullying, the pressure of working to externally imposed targets and the experience of constant surveillance.

Any new legislation, to be effective, would have to be buttressed by a strengthening of health and safety inspectorates, giving them the resources to respond to requests from trade unions and individuals to investigate breaches of minimum health and safety regulations and to initiate public awareness campaigns. It should be recognised here that – especially where the work involves provision of services to the public – issues of worker safety may be closely linked to consumer safety and public safety more generally. There is therefore a need to clarify which bodies are responsible, as well as for clear reporting procedures and realistic penalties for failures to comply.

Workers' rights should be spelled out in relation to obtaining information and reporting problems without being penalised. Clear rules should be set in place concerning insurance and legal liability and the procedures to be followed in case of accidents or work-related ill-health. Consultation around the development of this legislation could, with advantage, include revisiting past debates about whether it would be a good thing to set up a national occupational medical service linked to the NHS.

Further rights should address the risks to workers associated with algorithmic management. There is a need for clear rules concerning who has access to data about their work performance, who owns it, how it can be used, and workers' rights to see it, correct inaccuracies and have it deleted.

Linked with this should be a right to appeal against decisions made on the basis of the application of standard rules and algorithmically assisted decisions. In particular, there should be mechanisms for contesting hiring and recruitment decisions that may reflect algorithmic bias, for example on the basis of gender, ethnicity or disability. Similarly, it should be possible to contest algorithmically assisted suspension and termination of employment or withdrawal of payment, including decisions based on customer ratings.

Employers should be obliged to provide direct means of communication with workers that bypass those embedded in apps or websites, for example by providing a direct telephone hotline and/or an email address that is responded to by a human being within a certain time limit.

More broadly, any new legislation should revise and update other rights that, although they may still exist in law, have been inadequately defined in past legislation or chipped away at since the laws were originally enacted. These include such diverse issues as the rights of interns, responsibility for training and the certification of skills, and procedures for dealing with harassment, intimidation and discrimination at work.

This list is neither exhaustive nor definitive. What is important is firstly that the rights it refers to should be universal, and secondly that they should be accepted as reasonable and fair by a broad range of social constituencies representing the full spectrum of work in modern

Britain. These constituencies should therefore be closely involved in the detailed formulation of these demands to ensure their ownership and support. New workers' rights must also be linked closely with other demands for democratic reform, in a programme that links economic, social and civil rights, including trade union rights.

Generating a combined commitment to such a shared emancipatory programme, and a shared stake in bringing it into being amongst these diverse groups, could become a means of building new solidarities and strengthening old ones across the working class. Without such solidarities, there is a real risk that existing divisions among workers will be exacerbated.

IMPLEMENTATION AND ENFORCEMENT

However comprehensive a bill of workers' rights might be, it can only be effective if there are measures in place to ensure that these rights are properly enforced. At present, the obligations of employers and the rights of workers are embedded in a confusing hodge-podge of regulations, reinforced in different ways by a variety of different agencies, some operating at a national level and some specific to particular sectors, occupations, types of activity or localities.

Attaching conditions to licensing agreements

Before embarking on major legislative reforms affecting all employers and workers it is perhaps worth investigating the potential to expand the scope of existing licensing agreements and legal requirements and the extent to which they can be adapted to address current problems.

Some online platforms operate in fields that are already subject to licences and have mechanisms in place for attaching conditions to these licences and enforcing them through inspection regimes. One of the best-known examples of this is the licensing system for taxis in Greater London, enforced by Transport for London (TfL). At the time of writing, TfL has refused to grant Uber London a new private hire operator's licence in response to its latest application on the grounds that some of its practices put passenger safety at risk, although the company continues to operate in the city pending appeal.[5]

To take another example, there is also a plethora of regulations relating to the certification of skilled tradespeople such as electricians, plumbers and providers of building and maintenance services. Many of these workers are now employed via online platforms using a variety of different business models, some of which are very close indeed to implementing an employment relationship while others are more akin to online trade directories. While the employment status of the workers is murky, so too are a range of other issues relating to such questions as who is responsible for the health and safety of workers and clients, who is responsible for ensuring that workers are properly trained and certified, and who bears the cost of any legal action that may be taken in the event of an accident, a failure to deliver to the required standard, or another eventuality.

This could perhaps be addressed by requiring the relevant certifying bodies to amend their rules to introduce some clarity, but perhaps an easier solution would be to enforce standards by means of requiring such platforms to obtain a licence to operate and linking these licences to compulsory insurance schemes with specified obligations. Online platforms, or other employment intermediaries, could then be required by their insurance companies, as a condition of obtaining the insurance they need to secure their licence to operate, to demonstrate that they are following agreed guidelines in relation to health and safety, training and other relevant factors.

This would have to be done in a way that pins the responsibility for meeting these conditions onto the intermediary or platform which actually dictates the working conditions that determine health and safety. Responsibility should not be passed down the line to workers who may be forced to adopt unsafe practices by management pressure to meet targets.

Linking such conditions to the terms of insurance is a way of transferring to the market responsibilities for enforcement that would otherwise have to be carried out by overstretched public servants. Making insurance compulsory is not a new principle – it is used in other situations, for instance the requirement to have third party insurance before you are allowed to drive a car on a public highway.

The same principle could be applied across a range of other sectors, such as the provision of domestic cleaning.

Promoting good practice through local agreements

Another approach is to promote good practice through local agreements that can be enforced by local authorities through such means as withholding investment or denying access to opportunities to tender for outsourcing contracts.

An early example of this was the London Living Wage. The campaign began in East London in a grassroots movement that brought together churches, mosques, schools and other institutions, including trade unions. As early as 2004, at a public assembly, it secured a commitment that the Mayor of London would champion the idea of a living wage that would be substantially higher than the (then) national minimum wage and reflect the real cost of living in the nation's capital. Since then, the National Living Wage Foundation has developed a model by which employers agree voluntarily to becoming a Living Wage Employer, a model to which over 5,000 organisations have now signed up.[6] This commits them both to paying the 'real living wage' to all their directly employed staff and to encouraging their subcontractors to do so too. It is also possible for employers to become a 'recognised service provider' committed additionally to offering a living wage bid alongside every market rate submittal to all prospective and current clients, designed to encourage the linking of outsourcing contracts to a guarantee of decent wages.[7]

A more recent initiative is a bold plan by the Greater Manchester Combined Authority (GMCA) to prohibit zero-hours contracts as part of Manchester's 'Good Employment Charter'. Major early signatories include the Manchester Airports Group and Kellogg's, with over 100 companies in talks about joining the scheme. Joining is a condition for eligibility for investment from the Greater

Manchester Business Fund, which provides a strong incentive.[8]

Another local initiative, not yet implemented, comes from Hull, which has developed a proposal to trial UBI at a city level, echoing similar proposals from Sheffield, Liverpool and other members of the rapidly growing UBI Lab network.[9]

Changing national enforcement procedures

At present, the enforcement of workers' rights in the UK is scattered across a muddled patchwork of institutions, a situation that the government itself recognised as confusing when it launched a public consultation in 2019 about bringing them all together within a single enforcement body.[10] Minimum wage regulations are enforced by Her Majesty's Revenue and Customs (HMRC); regulations on labour exploitation and modern slavery by the Gangmasters and Labour Abuse Authority; the operations of employment agencies and employment businesses by the Employment Agency Standards Inspectorate; health and safety at work involving high risks by the Health and Safety Executive; and health and safety at work involving low risks by local authorities; rules concerning statutory payments (e.g. for sickness and maternity pay) by the HMRC Statutory Payments Disputes Team; and discriminatory practices by the Equality and Human Rights Commission.[11] To make matters even more confusing, many of the complaints that workers might have in the contemporary labour market (such as being arbitrarily dropped from an online platform, or subjected to discrimination as a result of algorithmic bias, or expected to spend long periods of unpaid time preparing and waiting for work), do not fall easily into any of these categories. Workers or their representatives seeking advice or conciliation in disputes can go to the Advisory, Conciliation and Arbitration Service (ACAS) or, if they want to take an employer to court, take their case to an Industrial Tribunal, for which, however, they are not eligible for legal aid.

Clearly there is an urgent need to simplify and rationalise this situation. However, amalgamating all these diverse services into a single agency might not be the best solution, despite its many apparent advantages. First, there is a risk of losing the considerable body of professional knowledge and expertise that has accumulated over the years in organisations like the Health and Safety Executive and ACAS. If the new combined agency is introduced in a standardised way, attempting to create a multi-skilled workforce that can deal with the whole range of issues, there is a risk that it could lead to the kinds of deskilling associated with similar attempts to amalgamate departments using a one-size-fits-all approach, and typically involving a 'callcenterisation'[12] of work processes. Research has shown that even where this is carried out with a high degree of staff involvement and good training, as in the Danish Tax and Customs Administration, it has nevertheless led to deprofessionalisation, deskilling, increased job dissatisfaction and higher staff turnover, bringing an overall loss of quality and expertise.[13]

Whether or not all the various agencies are formally brought under a single administrative umbrella, it seems likely that the best solution should involve a number of different elements.

The first of these would be a front-line information service, well-advertised and easy to access, to which workers can turn with their initial queries, with a similar parallel service for employers or labour market intermediaries. All workers should be provided with information about this first-tier service on hiring, and its contact details should be clearly displayed in any app that they are required to use associated with their work. The service should be offered in different languages and be available round the clock; its employees, in addition to supplying basic information, should also be able to provide a triage service (like the National Health Service's 111 helpline), passing the worker on, where needed, to a relevant expert who can offer specialist advice and, if need be, take the matter further on their behalf.

Second, there is a need for specialist legal and professional staff to provide a second-tier service, with job descriptions that are sufficiently broad to enable them to keep up with the latest research on how work is changing, act as mentors for new colleagues, provide training for first-tier front-line staff, disseminate information to workers, employers and labour market intermediaries through publications and websites, and organise workshops and other such activities as well as advising central and local government.

Third, there is a need for teams of inspectors operating at a local level, who can carry out direct inspections and have the power to investigate local businesses or local branches of national and international businesses. In addition to liaising with the second-tier staff described above, they would also be available, when needed, to be called on by the first-tier triage service to investigate cases on their patch. These on-the-spot enforcement staff could also collaborate with other local bodies, including trade unions, chambers of commerce, legal and administrative institutions and organisations providing information, counselling or other forms of support to workers to provide a joined-up local service to workers.

If other examples of the reorganisation of public services are anything to go by, the most likely neoliberal 'new public management' solution to this problem would be the implementation of the first of these elements, but with few resources going to the second or the third. It must be emphasised that any genuine improvement in the enforcement of workers' rights will be impossible unless it is backed up on the one hand by strong professional expertise and on the other by well-resourced local enforcement teams.

CONCLUSIONS

This chapter has looked at the erosion of workers' rights and the need for a new universal charter of rights to protect them. After reviewing some of the elements that should be included in such a charter, it turned its attention to how these rights might be enforced, concluding that there are a variety of means available but that these can only be effective if properly resourced. It notes that these do not in all cases necessarily have to emanate from central government but that there is considerable scope for local action. The development of bottom-up local initiatives is the focus of the next chapter.

CHAPTER EIGHT

Digital Platforms for Public Good

The solutions I have proposed so far would go some way towards addressing the problems identified in chapters 2 and 3, helping to construct a welfare state that provides a social safety net and decent employment in line with the underlying objectives of the twentieth-century model and the principles of fair redistribution and universal access to benefits and services. But if we want a welfare state fit for the twenty-first century we need to go further, to address the concerns raised in chapter 4 relating to gender equality and the provision of care to an ageing population, as well as the other great challenges facing the whole planet, most notably the challenge of the climate emergency.

THE AMBIVALENT CHARACTER OF TECHNOLOGY

In this chapter I step into some less charted territory and make proposals for using the new digital technologies not just to enhance and expand existing welfare services but also to bring into being entirely new services that can contribute to the development of a new kind of welfare state: one that not only provides its citizens with the basic services they need for decent lives but also contributes in new ways to the improvement of work-life balance for both women and men, the creation of jobs with decent wages and working conditions and the strengthening of local economies, while also reducing waste and energy consumption.

This entails a radical rethink of attitudes to digital technologies among groups that have up to now been rightly critical of their negative social, economic and environmental impacts. I do not start from the simplistic position that technologies are necessarily neutral.

It is obvious that many technologies can be used equally for socially productive or destructive purposes. A knife can be used to prepare food or to kill somebody. Social media can be used to overcome social isolation and generate new friendships or to harass and bully. Helicopters can be used to get sick people to hospital quickly or to rain down bullets on defenceless civilians. Notwithstanding this duality, technologies may additionally also be biased in their very design to serve the interests of the dominant groups in society who commission, purchase and use them, and can often be seen to incorporate values that help to consolidate that dominance to the disadvantage of more vulnerable groups. This can be illustrated by the ways that data collected from consumers and workers may be used to target them for sales or manipulate them into particular forms of behaviour. Nevertheless, all technologies are produced by human ingenuity and human labour, and the human beings who design these systems to serve the needs of their current masters are, under the right circumstances, quite capable of redesigning them for other purposes in the service of different masters, with different priorities and values.

DOWNSIDES OF ONLINE PLATFORMS IN THEIR CURRENT FORMS

The research I undertook into online platforms points to some serious disadvantages to workers and other users in the ways that they currently operate. First, they tend to be owned by large international corporations that pay little or no tax and put nothing back into the communities in which they operate beyond the (usually very low) earnings that accrue to the workers. Not only do these companies fail to contribute to local economies, they actively damage them, hoovering out a percentage of the value of each transaction (typically 20–25 per cent) so that it accrues elsewhere: a value that would previously have remained in the pocket of an independent worker and been spent in the local economy may now be enriching a company in California.

Second, online platforms are associated with the exploitation of vulnerable workers. This does not just impact negatively on the lives of the workers directly affected; its effects ripple more broadly across the economy, undercutting the wages and conditions of workers employed by more traditional firms operating in the same fields and contributing to a general spread of precarious working.

I could point to other detrimental effects but these two are enough to be going on with. Neither is of course unique to online platforms. There is a long history of corporate tax-dodging and exploitation of vulnerable workers among companies that have nothing to do with digital technologies. Nevertheless, it is undoubtedly the case that the exponential expansion of online platforms, and particularly the ease with which they can hop across national borders without having to make any investment in bricks and mortar or heavy machinery, has been greatly assisted by digitalisation. Added to this has been a reluctance on the part of many policymakers to limit their growth, because new applications of technology represent 'innovation' and may lead to the creation of new jobs. Nevertheless, and this is the point that must be emphasised, there is nothing *intrinsic* to the use of the digital technologies that power online platforms that *necessarily* leads to these socially and economically harmful effects.

REPURPOSING PLATFORM TECHNOLOGIES FOR PUBLIC GOOD – STARTING LOCALLY

What if these technologies could be repurposed, under different forms of ownership and with different objectives governing their design, into instruments for achieving social and economic good? Chapter 4 showed a diagram illustrating the role of online platforms and precarious work in the development of a miserable vicious cycle whereby time poverty and financial poverty chase each other in an ever-intensifying squeeze on the quality of daily life, like the legendary ouroboros devouring its own tail. Could these very same technologies be used to reverse this cycle? This is the idea I explore in the rest of this chapter.

Unlike some of the other ideas discussed in previous chapters, the best place to start in developing experiments to find positive uses for platform technologies is not to introduce them from above, via central government initiatives, but, on the contrary, to root them in local communities where a range of stakeholders can come together laterally to develop solutions that take all their needs into account, solutions that they have some ownership of and commitment to, and that are democratically accountable to local residents.

This is the approach advocated by, among others, Hilary Cottam, whose book *Radical Help* argues eloquently that the neoliberal state, with its 'new public management' bureaucratic approach, is incapable of delivering solutions that meet people's real needs.[1] Her alternative approach is based on recognising capabilities, developing relationships, building horizontal bridges between different organisations and remaining open to new developments. She gives examples of several local experiments in which this method has been adopted, tackling problems relating to such varied issues as social care, health, job search, education and services for the elderly.

It is precisely because of the importance of such local, collaborative, bottom-up approaches that the rest of this chapter does not present worked-out blueprints but rather a series of suggestions designed to form a starting point for open discussions at a local level – discussions that could lead to imaginative solutions tailored to local circumstances and to which local people can be actively committed, having been consulted about their development and actively involved in making them work.

For the same reason, I have not been prescriptive about how such initiatives might be organised or funded. There are many different options in each case, and how any new public or public-private platforms could be developed and managed is a matter for debate, consultation and experimentation. They will almost certainly require a kind of joined-up thinking that links services previously provided separately. In doing so, they will be in tune with current progressive ideas that seek, for example, to integrate health and care services, requiring new forms of co-operation between the NHS and local authorities. In some cities and regions they would be able to build on existing inter-agency partnerships, such as the Greater Manchester Health and Social Care partnership which includes 35 different borough councils, NHS Foundation Trusts, Clinical Commissioning Groups and other bodies, such as the regional ambulance service.[2]

It is possible that setting up entirely new bodies might be the best solution in some cases. Alternatively there is scope for new kinds of partnership between different public entities, private sector organisations (such as technology providers), voluntary organisations and other bodies, such as co-operatives. It would be useful here to have a variety of different pilot schemes that could be evaluated independently.

The success of any such schemes should be judged by a range of criteria including cost, efficiency, how well they meet the needs of users, how open they are to democratic scrutiny and the extent to which user groups, workers and the bodies that represent them are actively involved in their design and implementation. Where services are complementing existing public provision, for example, it is particularly important to have the active and constructive involvement of public sector trade unions, to avoid the schemes inadvertently becoming a means of undermining existing collective agreements or casualising the workforce. If new workers are to be recruited to help deliver new public services it is important that their terms and conditions of employment match those of existing public sector workers. Thought should also be given to their training, skills certification and career development.

The most important thing, in my view, is to avoid conflicts between different local stakeholders and to find the best consensus that is acceptable to all parties. In some cases this might mean starting slowly with small pilot schemes, taking baby steps towards larger schemes while people get used to the idea of change, assess their impact and identify any unintended consequences, while leaving open options for further adjustment.

TRANSPORT SERVICES

One field in which online platforms have already made a dramatic impact is in transport services. Companies like Uber and Bolt have posed a major competitive threat to established taxi and minicab services, driving some out of the market altogether while forcing others to change their practices to make them more like online platforms in how they operate. Outside major cities like London, their expansion has also been driven by cuts in other forms of transport, such as buses.

Meanwhile, with the growth of online shopping, the privatisation of previously national postal services around the world and the incursion of new, low-cost courier companies, some using platform models, an intense competition has grown up for the delivery of goods along the 'last mile',[3] driving a race to the bottom in wages and conditions for the increasingly casualised workers whose job it is to get packages to customers as quickly and cheaply as possible. There is a growing convergence here between the delivery of items that might previously have been handled by the postal service and that of other items, such as ready meals and supermarket shopping, that might formerly have been picked up in person by the customer or delivered by staff directly employed by retailers or fast food chains.

The impacts of these developments on local communities are multiple. There are more vehicles on the roads, meaning more pollution and greater consumption of fossil fuels. There is a growing pool of underpaid, precarious workers whose poor and stressed-out families are more likely to be a burden on local services and less able to contribute positively to the local economy. The global platforms and logistics companies they work for are sucking out value from this local economy while putting little back in by way of taxes and wages. Meanwhile, the very structure of the local urban landscape is being transformed. While retailers on the high streets are driven out of business, large suburban warehouses may be being replaced by smaller local depots or pick-up points in the inner city.[4] The extension of food delivery networks, driven by the algorithms used by platforms such as Deliveroo and Uber Eats, is leading to the development of 'dark kitchens' situated at a distance from their parent restaurants but designed to be close to potential customers. Often these are in converted shipping containers with inadequate heating and ventilation, situated in car parks, providing very poor working conditions for the chefs.[5] Such developments not only affect the rest of the local transport sector but also reconfigure urban space and change the character of neighbourhoods.

Yet, as already noted, the technologies that underpin the online platforms do not necessarily or inevitably lead to these negative consequences. The algorithms that power the platforms allow supply and demand for services to be matched in real time. Under present conditions, this generally requires workers to be available on call to supply the services at short notice without any guarantee of work or payment. Having to wait in their own time for a task to be allocated is one of the worst aspects of platform work. But there is no reason for the supply of labour necessarily to be organised in this way. It is perfectly possible for workers to be fully paid to work clearly defined shifts and still be available to be redeployed flexibly on demand. Indeed, this is the way that most emergency services currently operate, as well as a range of other services such as the repair of malfunctioning infrastructure or appliances. In fact the larger the workforce the easier it is to ensure that there are always people on duty without requiring last-minute shift changes or expecting some workers to be on call – especially if staffing levels are set on a 'just-in-case' rather than a 'just-in-time' principle. With the supply of labour organised in this way, it becomes much easier to respond flexibly to demands for services without exploiting the workforce – while still giving workers a choice in which hours they work.

Under different forms of management and ownership, platform technologies could be used not only to improve working conditions but also to benefit local communities in other ways. For example, intelligent planning and a reduction in competition would make it possible to optimise the deployment of drivers, reducing the number of vehicles on the road at any given time, and thereby also reducing energy consumption and pollution as well as costs.

Here are just a few ideas for ways in which platform technologies could contribute to improved transport policies at a local level.

Integration with other transport services

One possibility would be to see individual taxi journeys not as in competition with existing public transport services but as complementary to them. For example, Uber-type services could be used to transport people with disabilities from their homes to stations where they can connect with (suitably adapted) train or bus services, helping to maximise the use of these collective forms of public transport and reduce the use of cars for longer journeys.

Local online transport platforms could also be used to supplement ambulance services to transport people to and from medical appointments or day-care services on demand, without the need for inflexible advance booking systems. With appropriately trained and vetted staff they could also be used to transport children with special needs to and from school or after-school facilities.

There is no reason why transport services provided free to those in need could not be combined with paid-for services, perhaps by using a voucher system for the free trips. This would deliver economies of scale and help with the rational planning of services, as well as making it possible for some cross-subsidy from paying customers to those eligible for free transport. If they were receiving the same level of convenience and service that they obtained previously from a private platform, it is likely that many people would choose to use a publicly or collectively managed one, in the knowledge that the portion of the fare that previously went to the global platform provider was now being spent on providing decent employment for local people, with the extra value created remaining in the local economy. Thus, for example, the vehicles that transport children to and from school could also be made available as a paid-for service to other households, reducing school-run congestion and private car use.

Centralised purchasing of vehicles for use by these alternative platforms would make it possible to ensure high environmental standards, for example by using only electric cars.

A local strategy for reorganising the 'last mile'

Many people and organisations delivering goods to homes and businesses play a contributory role in the jams of traffic clogging our streets. There are individuals on cycles, scooters or in cars, each carrying a single item such as an important document, a pizza, or a life-saving sample of blood, sometimes bearing the logo of a courier company such as City Sprint, or a food delivery platform such as Deliveroo or Uber Eats. Then there are vans delivering packages sent via Royal Mail, or via its now-privatised competitors from other countries such as the German DHL or the Dutch TNT, not to mention the (always commercial) American UPS. Added to these are newer entrants to the market such as Hermes and Yodel. Many retailers, both online and offline, organise their own deliveries, so residential streets are also thronged with vehicles sporting the logos of companies like John Lewis, Ocado, Tesco and Sainsburys.

The incentives to customers to pick up their own goods from designated collection points testify to the difficulty of making a profit in these competitive circumstances. So, might there be an inducement to persuade at least some corporate customers to buy into alternative arrangements – arrangements that would rationalise the logistics of these multiple deliveries and reduce the number of vehicles on the road while offering decent local employment? Would it, for example, be possible for local authorities to encourage the development of a single unified fleet of delivery vehicles (using energy-efficient vehicles and employing drivers with decent working conditions), perhaps supplemented by cyclists, offering a delivery service within a designated area to take advantage of economies of scale, picking up from all local depots and delivering to all local residents using a platform-based organisational model? If it were possible to renationalise the Royal Mail and make it locally accountable and integrated with other traffic management schemes, then this might be an alternative route to the same end, but under the present government such a development seems unlikely.

A combination of carrots and sticks could be used to encourage take up, such as offering planning concessions to companies operating good employment practices in their warehouse management, restricting loading and unloading by vehicles that are likely to be polluting, or refusal of licences to companies that do not conform to good practices. Encouraging customers to use designated collection points to pick up their goods is of course environmentally beneficial, but there will always be people who are unable to do this, for instance because they are disabled or unable to leave the home due to their caring commitments. A more integrated and joined-up system would make it possible for a public courier service to pick up goods from the nearest collection point, rather than the warehouse of origin, dramatically reducing the amount of driving or riding time per delivery, while still ensuring that they are brought to the door.

CARE SERVICES

Perhaps one of the greatest challenges facing us as we enter the third decade of the twenty-first century is how to restore and improve our existing public services, and to do so with a dual aim: to counter the effects of austerity, and to reverse the fragmentation and bureaucratisation of these services related to the perverse management practices necessitated by breaking their delivery down into separate units that can profitably be outsourced to private companies (while leaving the public authorities responsible for any risks that arise).

At a time of major growth in demand for health and care services due to the ageing population, many services (such as meals-on-wheels, hospital transport and respite care) have been cut altogether or reduced to standardised formats. One example of the latter is the standard 15 minutes allowed for home care visits. This fails to meet the needs of users, some of whom may be able to manage fine without a visit at all on some days, but require much longer and more intensive attention on others, often unpredictably. It also puts intolerable strains on the workforce, who have to dash from appointment to appointment, caught between their altruistic desire to do the job well by attending to the needs of their clients, and the management-imposed imperative to meet their targets at all costs.

As already noted, there is no reason why the technologies used to order a private taxi could not also be used to organise transport to day centres or hospital appointments for those unable to use public transport. Similarly, the technologies that make it possible to order food to be delivered at short notice via a phone app could equally be used to supply ready meals for the housebound and elderly. Even more importantly, there is no reason why the technologies used to summon supermarket checkout operators or wait staff to the branch of the supermarket or coffee chain where their skills are needed could not also be used to get domestic care workers to their clients at a mutually agreeable time. Indeed, there are already a number of online platforms that claim to provide private care services to households on this basis, such as care.com, which provides care for the elderly but also for children and pets, and childcare.co.uk, which provides babysitting services.

In the hands of clever and publicly accountable technicians, technological solutions could be found for many problems. If it is possible for existing commercial platforms to target individual users with special offers (such as two-for-one special deals, or discounts if you introduce a friend to the service), then surely it is not beyond the capability of these technicians to design, for example, a voucher system that allocates a certain number of hours of care over a set period to a particular user, with a graduated system of charges kicking in if this is exceeded.

Local care platforms

One possibility might be to develop local platforms for the provision of care work, perhaps in partnership or collaboration with existing care providers. Bringing together the relevant local stakeholders to discuss more flexible alternatives might throw up solutions that would not only give the patient more autonomy but also allow workers to put in the amount of time actually required for any given visit. For example, instead of trying to second-guess how many care appointments might be needed, why not have an app that makes it possible for vulnerable users and the partners or relatives caring for them at home to ask for help when (and only when) they actually need it?

A lot of practical details would of course have to be ironed out to make such systems feasible but they might actually be easier to solve than the problems local authorities are already grappling with trying to make ever-scarcer resources available to an ever-expanding and needier population of people needing social care. Here we should not just consider the elderly and long-term disabled who make up such a high proportion of existing clients for social care, but also the short-term care of people newly discharged from hospital who may only need help over a short period while they recuperate.

As with other services, combining free care for those entitled to receive it from the state with paid-for services would allow for economies of scale, making it possible to set staffing levels that reduce stress for care workers and maximise their choice of shift patterns to fit with their personal lives and schedules. The precise matching of supply and demand enabled by platform technologies would also generate efficiencies, for example by reducing missed appointments.

Integration of health and care services

Online platforms could also play a role in helping to support the integration of health and social care services at a local level. For example they would make it easier to coordinate the timing of home visits from different health and care professionals, to share practical information such as dates of hospital appointments or discharges, to arrange the timing of check-ups with dentists, opticians or audiologists, and, in collaboration with local pharmacies, to organise the delivery of repeat prescriptions. If well-managed, such services could support hard-pressed local General Practitioner services and reinforce their role as central agents in a joined-up service.

Childcare

It would also be possible to use this approach for other care services, such as childcare. Imagine what a boon it would be for harassed single parents to have a certain number of hours of free childcare (provided, of course, by vetted, certified experts) per year to deal with emergencies? Again, the maximum benefits from such a scheme would arise if free publicly provided services were combined with paid-for ones. The greater the critical mass, the greater the possibility for offering a wide range of choices to users and the higher the possibility of being able to offer workers the shift choices that suit them.

A publicly provided service would have other advantages. At the simplest level, by eliminating the profit currently taken by online platforms, it would reduce the cost and enable resources to be deflected towards improving employment standards and staff benefits. It could also be managed in such a way that it is not obvious which customer is paying what, thus avoiding any stigma associated with being in receipt of free services. Furthermore, it makes it possible to offer different degrees of support tailored to the needs of individual households. Finally, it could establish high standards of safety and professionalism and, as a public body, be accountable to local communities.

DOMESTIC SERVICES

Decades of feminist research have demonstrated that probably the single most crucial obstacle to equality for women is the 'housework problem', whereby women do disproportionately more unpaid care and household maintenance work than men, which in turn affects not only their roles in the household but also their ability to participate in paid employment outside the home. Of course, digitalisation in and of itself cannot free women from carrying an unfair share of the load of unpaid domestic work. However by offering a new range of services, affordable even to the poorest by being linked into the welfare system, online platforms could help to free up the time of both women and men and offer new choices for dealing with such things as childcare, caring and cooking for the sick and elderly, and cleaning. If these services were provided on a flexible just-in-time basis, they could be used even by people with awkward and unpredictable shift patterns, or dealing with fluctuating health conditions. In doing so, they would make a direct contribution to liberation from the necessity of performing these tasks. When combined with progressive and innovative public policies to provide a basic subsistence income, and with fair employment policies that respect the rights of both female and male workers, public service platforms could help ensure that women and men can access the labour market on more equal terms, while improving their work-life balance.

Public household service platforms

I have mentioned the possibility of combining free and paid-for services in the context of transport and care services. In relation to other domestic services, such as cleaning and help with household maintenance, this becomes even more important because the relationship between time poverty and need on the one hand, and money poverty on the other, is not a symmetrical one. The chances are that the greater your need for help with housework the less likely you are to have the money to pay for it.

Online platforms, with their ability to make sophisticated distinctions among clients, open up the possibility of redistribution between households to make this situation fairer. There are many possible ways to do this. One model might be to offer a certain number of free hours of help in situations of demonstrable need, for example in households with young children, or where a disabled person is being cared for, assessment for which could be linked to other benefits. An alternative might be to have graduated charges related to differing personal circumstances. Another possibility could be a voucher scheme. It might be very helpful, for example, on discharge from hospital after debilitating surgery, in the first months after childbirth, or while undergoing a course of chemotherapy, to be awarded vouchers for a certain number of free sessions to get you through a difficult period.

Local businesses could also play a part. For example, employers who require certain workers to work awkward shift patterns could reward them with domestic service vouchers, or bundle services in with maternity and paternity leave packages.

As with other forms of personal service, the greater the usage of the platform the greater the scope for economies of scale and, alongside this, of improving working conditions for the workforce.

Integration with other services

Housework involves a range of different tasks including cleaning, maintenance, shopping, food preparation and care work. Domestic services could therefore be integrated with other services in a wide range of different configurations. They could, for example, be provided in partnership with existing suppliers of elder-care services, childcare services, cleaning services, household maintenance services, shopping services or food delivery services.

It is quite possible that there is no single best way of organising these services. Ideally each locality should be able to come up with its own solution, using a bottom-up approach in which local stakeholders are brought together to brainstorm and decide what will work best for their own community, building on existing strengths. Successful pilot schemes could then be rolled out more broadly.

Organisationally speaking, it seems likely that the most important priority will be to ensure that any solution is accountable to local citizens. This might involve resisting attempts to impose top-down solutions either from national or international companies or agencies or from central government. It would mean giving priority to horizontal local networks over vertical ones, in which there is a risk of standard one-size-fits-all models being imposed from above, not only depriving local people of the choice to determine their own priorities but also risking a situation where the added value of these services does not accrue fully to the workers who provide them and the residents who receive them.

FOOD SERVICES

I have already mentioned using the model of food delivery platforms as a basis for providing 'meals-on-wheels' for disabled or elderly housebound people unable to shop or cook for themselves. However, integrating food provision into social care services is only one model. Food delivery could alternatively, or additionally, be integrated within a broader local food strategy.

In some parts of Britain, local authorities are already developing imaginative local food plans. One example of this is Bristol, which has developed a 'good food plan' for the city.[6] This originated in a local initiative involving a diverse range of stakeholders including local government, community-based and business organisations.[7] Its ambitious aims include transforming Bristol's food culture, encouraging the diversity of food retail, safeguarding land for food production, increasing urban food production, redistributing, recycling and composting food waste, protecting key infrastructure for local food supplies, increasing market opportunities for local and regional suppliers and supporting community food enterprises.[8]

Efficient distribution plays a key role in any such local strategy, not least because getting perishable goods to where they are needed quickly is important for reducing waste and ensuring high quality.

The more precise matching of supply and demand enabled by digital technologies is crucial here. This is something that will improve as networks grow, multiplying the options and introducing economies of scale. Integrated local networks, managed online, could have the potential to link together a wide range of different suppliers and consumers in local supply chains. They could also open up markets for local producers, to the benefit of the local economy.

Just as it is possible for small-scale energy producers to supply energy to the national grid when they have a surplus, an effective local network could make it possible to link in very small-scale food suppliers, such as allotment holders, co-operatives or small enterprises making artisanal foods, to distribute their products and prevent surplus food going to waste in times of glut.

Improving food supply to local institutions

Local food networks could make it easier to ensure a supply of nutritious, sustainably produced food to local institutions such as schools, hospitals, residential care homes, prisons, universities or work canteens, either in the form of fresh raw materials to be cooked on site or as pre-prepared ready meals. They could, for example, contribute to the development of the more sustainable food policies advocated by the Department of Health,[9] making greater use of local suppliers and thus reducing the cost and carbon footprint of transport as well as increasing freshness.

Avoiding waste while addressing hunger

Following examples such as that of the Oxford Food Bank,[10] surplus food could be collected from wholesalers, supermarkets and restaurants for distribution to charities, local kitchens or market stalls via these networks. Apart from its clear social value in addressing food poverty and redistributing food, this also has the added benefit of reducing waste. A coordinated network could contribute to a local sustainable waste management strategy by other means too, for example by ensuring that food waste is transferred efficiently to composting services, and decreasing the amount of food spoilage caused by delays in over-long or inefficiently managed supply chains.

Home delivery of food

I have already mentioned the home delivery of food in the context of reinventing meals-on-wheels and providing services to time-strapped households. However, integrating it with care services is only one option. It could equally be linked more firmly into the local ecosystem of shops, restaurants and cafes, providing an alternative to, or extension of, existing food delivery platform services. Whether they involve supplying freshly cooked food (as in platforms like Deliveroo or Uber Eats) or frozen ready meals (as supplied by companies like Wiltshire Farm Foods, cookfood.net or various supermarket chains), one of the great attractions of these new services, as compared with traditional institutional meals-on-wheels services, is the much greater range of choices available to customers.

A local food network would be able to provide such choice, for example by linking in suppliers of traditional ethnic cuisines, vegan or vegetarian options, or foods for people with specific dietary needs (such as those with coeliac disease or diabetes or on a weight-loss regime).

In the process, it could support local restaurants or other food-producing businesses while also ensuring a good range of cultural and nutritional choice for users. The 'dark kitchens' model could even be used by local authorities as a means of providing support for new food enterprises in the start-up phase. With control over the planning process, they would be able to provide for suitable premises that meet health and safety standards in the right locations. This could be a good way to help people from migrant communities put their traditional culinary skills to productive use. Not only could this support the start up of new businesses, it could also extend the range of cuisines available to local communities.

As in other cases, subsidised options combined with paid-for ones would help to generate critical mass. Wouldn't it be nice, for example, to come out of hospital in the knowledge that you have a few vouchers for free meals from your favourite kitchen to use during your recovery period? Or for parents in poverty to know that their children will have at least one nutritious cooked meal per day during the school holidays?

From dark kitchens to bright restaurants

There is no reason why food networks should be used only to deliver food from remote kitchens to people's homes. The direction could also be reversed, by using them to deliver ingredients or prepared food to places where the food can be eaten communally. Affordable community restaurants can be a vital resource for the homeless. They can also help break down loneliness and bring together people who would otherwise be isolated in their homes, for example because of mental illness or poverty. They could complement, or substitute for, food banks, providing places where parents who lack proper cooking facilities can bring their children for nutritious cooked meals. Setting up dispersed networks of affordable restaurants in areas of food need would not just help the immediate recipients but also contribute to revitalising high streets by repurposing empty shop premises for these purposes. Again, there is no reason why low-cost meals for those in need should not be cross-subsidised by higher prices charged to customers who can afford to pay more.

ONLINE LABOUR EXCHANGES FOR THE SELF-EMPLOYED

The platform model need not be restricted to the supply of household or transport services. It could also be used to supply other forms of labour in a way that boosts local economies. For example instead of going to a platform like Fiverr, or Upwork or PeoplePerHour to find, say, a free-lance graphic designer or a translator, it might be possible to use a locally based not-for-profit platform to search for such a person. Many individuals and businesses would probably be happy to do so in the knowledge that the work is going to people who live locally and will spend their earnings in the local economy, thus helping other local businesses, and that any commission taken by the platform is being spent on its maintenance and further development and the training and insurance of workers, rather than being taken as profit.

The development of such platforms could be boosted by encouraging local organisations to use them as their first port of call. For example they could be named as preferred suppliers of IT, translation, design or information services to local hospitals, police forces or other institutions. Businesses tendering to supply services to the local authority could be asked to use them in preference to global suppliers.

Such platforms would also be in a position to support the self-employed people registered on them in securing their rights to such things as pay rates that conform with living wage requirements, health and safety, trade union representation and ownership of the intellectual property they have produced. Once they have achieved sufficient scale, these platforms would also be able to set up exemplary schemes for providing benefits such as pensions and maternity, paternity or sick leave for the self-employed, as well as collaborate with local training institutions to provide work opportunities for their graduates and help them into self-employment through initiatives such as mentoring schemes.

PREFIGURATIVE MODELS

During the coronavirus crisis in 2020, there has been an enormous upsurge in collaborative activity to support vulnerable groups in local communities, much of it organised online. People have come together to make and distribute personal protective equipment, to shop for neighbours isolated in their homes, to cook and distribute food, to support vulnerable children, to provide emergency accommodation, supplies for the homeless and emotional support for the mentally ill. This suggests that there is strong potential for a willingness to participate in further bottom-up initiatives in the future.

Even more importantly, the crisis has triggered a new wave of thinking outside the box. Alongside unprecedented challenges to the racism that permeates British society, it has also encouraged a renewed interest in economic and social alternatives, including demands for a UBI.

CONCLUSIONS

This chapter has sketched out some ideas for potential uses of online platform technologies to bring about a positive redistribution of social resources, improve existing welfare services and develop new services at a local level. Many of these services go beyond the aims of the twentieth-century welfare state by addressing feminist and green demands explicitly. They thus contribute to the development of a broader socialist vision. I have avoided making specific prescriptive demands, which would thwart the intention of ensuring that new services are produced in a bottom-up way that responds to the needs of local communities, and, once developed, remain accountable to these local communities and open to change by them. They are intended not as a blueprint but to stimulate local discussion and inspire the development of local solutions.

CHAPTER NINE

The Way Forward

This book started with an analysis of the way that the welfare state model established in the mid twentieth century with the ambitious goal of creating a more equal society has morphed into its opposite. It has become, overwhelmingly, a vehicle for redistributing not from the rich to the poor but from the poor to the rich, and instead of providing workers with basic rights and a dignified life has turned into a means of humiliating and harassing them and bullying them into jobs that are precarious and unsafe. Furthermore, this welfare state has failed spectacularly both to deliver genuine equality of opportunity for women and to address the climate emergency meaningfully.

Those who care about equality, liberty, freedom from want, and the future of the planet are confronted with enormous challenges. How can we reverse the direction of redistribution, restore the principle of universality and, even more importantly, reinvent the welfare state to address the needs of women and the future sustainability of life on this earth?

THE IMPORTANCE OF THE NATION STATE

In the twentieth century, the answer to this question seemed to lie with national governments. But in the twenty-first, in the context of globalisation, the assumption that everything can be solved at a national level has become enormously problematic. We have to acknowledge, however, that the idea of a strong nation state remains appealing to large sections of the population, as became evident in the debates about Brexit. For many, there was a conflation between membership of the European Single Market (of which the UK was a member from 1973 to 2020) and the global spread of neoliberalism with which this membership more or less coincided.

European institutions, like national governments around the world, could be regarded as complicit in neoliberal policies. But this complicity ought not to be confused with causality. During this period there was indeed a burgeoning of standardisation and regulation and a more or less continuous process of institutional restructuring, with bewildering acronyms replacing one another at a pace dictated, it seemed, by the need to ensure that no organisational innovation stayed in place long enough for anyone actually to be held accountable for it. But these are part of the very mechanisms by which neoliberal policies are enacted, with complex mutual dependencies, tensions and interactions between global corporations, national governments, supra-national bodies, consultancies and lobbies. These intersections are visible not just in the intersecting cogs of the various bureaucracies but in the movements of individuals between these spheres (e.g. former ministers sitting on corporate boards and former CEOs advising governments).

Although Brussels represents a particularly dense node in this ecosystem it is better viewed – like national governments – as a site of negotiation and conflict between different economic and political actors than as an autonomously functioning source of power. In other words, the EU is not itself to blame for globalisation or for neoliberalism, though it has played a role in the mutual shaping of global capitalism and of individual human subjects.

Leaving this supra-national institution and reverting to a form of government in which the national level is the top one does not address the problem of globalisation. Those who dislike the changes that have taken place since 1973 are deluded if they imagine that the clock can be turned back to return us to a Britain with coherent communities, shared values and 'sovereignty': a world in which you can leave your door unlocked at night and hear only English spoken on the buses, in which trade unions get together with the CBI for cosy talks at 10 Downing Street over beer and sandwiches, Commonwealth countries are grateful for their independence, immigrants and women know their place, The Beatles are playing on the radio and Morecambe and Wise on the telly. A world where you knew where you were, when fuel bills were paid to the local electricity and gas boards, telephones were installed by British Telecom and you did not have to do confusing research to organise a pension or an insurance policy or remember a pin number to access what was yours.

The hard reality is that this world has gone, along with the Beveridgean welfare state in its twentieth-century form. In or out of the EU, we now live in a world where Apple, Facebook and Uber hold sway, where jobs are fragmented into discrete tasks, cultures are trivialised and commercialised, and populations, increasingly regarded as consumers rather than citizens, are atomised and set competitively against each other in global markets.

The idea of a bounded national state, all-powerful within its own borders, is certainly attractive to many elements on the right of the political spectrum, who invoke it as a means of closing the borders to immigrants and expelling those already settled here, as well as rolling back reforms enshrined in international conventions and European directives that commit governments to granting basic human rights, formal equality between the sexes and workers' rights.

A not dissimilar position, however, can also be found on the left, where many express a romantic attachment to the idea of the nation state as a natural unit of government which, once seized, whether through the ballot box or by revolution, could make possible an alternative political system, a 'socialism in one country', bringing justice and equality. This notion has a huge common-sense logical appeal. You identify where the power is (whether military power, the power to extract taxes or the power to make laws) and then you seize control. And bingo you have a people's government. For many that source of power has seemed to be the nation state, and if you happen to be a full citizen of that state this is not so problematic, though it may seem more so if you are a migrant without citizen-ship rights, if your identity is that of a culturally defined minority (such as being Jewish or Roma), if you are the resident of a former colony whose borders were imposed by the colonial power, or in even more conflicted circum-stances, for example in European regions such as Wales, Bosnia, Catalunya or Lapland. Because it is where much power still resides, as well as being the only territory over which one can win control legitimately and peacefully in democratic elections, the nation state is the obvious focus of political attention and the level at which policies must be made.

It therefore stands at the centre of a large conundrum. Capturing the nation state remains the major goal of any political party, and its legislative power is essential to enact new policies. Yet its powers to deliver change are quite limited in a world in which so many of the major decisions that shape our daily lives are taken by international companies based elsewhere in the world – companies such as Facebook or Google that control the information we access, Apple or Microsoft that determine how we access that information and how we work, Amazon that controls our purchasing and how the goods reach us, the international telecoms, energy and water companies that provide us with basic services, the global outsourcing companies that increasingly deliver our public services ... the list could go on. And it should be noted that these global corporations increasingly follow a business model that does not simply sell us a commodity and then quit the scene – they charge a rent. In order to continue to use their services, the individual citizen has to continue paying for them in instalments. Regular bills for electricity, gas or phone charges are now supplemented by regular bills to continue to use a software licence, watch films on Sky or Netflix, get 'prime' deliveries or obtain maintenance on increasingly complicated household appliances. Every time we use a platform like Uber or Airbnb, a percentage of what we pay goes to a global company – under conditions that can be arbitrarily changed without consultation or consent. Such platforms are thus not only determining the conditions of daily life but are also extorting payments – tithes or rents that may total more than we pay to our own governments in taxes.

How can a single nation state act even to persuade such companies to pay their fair share of tax let alone break up their monopolies or compel them to act in ethical ways? A politics that focuses only on the national level is clearly inadequate, yet policies introduced at that level are a necessary precondition for progress.

LESSONS FROM THE 2019 UK GENERAL ELECTION

The 2019 UK general election provided striking evidence that the current political system is inadequate to deal with these contradictions. There are several dimensions to this problem.

The first relates to competing and incompatible notions of democracy – with the referendum pitted against parliamentary democracy. The referendum follows a logic that decrees that once a vote has been taken 'the people have spoken' and the outcome should stand indefinitely. Parliamentary democracy works on the basis that people change their minds and it is to be expected that any vote might produce a different result from the previous one. Furthermore, the electorate vote for an individual politician who will make decisions on their behalf in response to unpredictable events, guided by whatever information and professional advice is available at the time. If they do not like the decisions taken, people are free to vote for somebody else next time round. When these two logics come into conflict with each other, as they did in 2019, an enormous amount of anger and mutual hostility is generated among supporters of each system, not only making rational debate difficult but also forcing voting patterns that prioritise arguments about what constitutes 'true democracy' over other political considerations.

The second dimension of the problem relates to the inability of the first-past-the-post electoral system to deal adequately with a situation where there are more than two parties with significant membership and where there are strong differences of opinion on certain key issues within, as well as between, parties. In the 2019 election not only were two different binary logics in play (Conservative vs Labour and pro-Brexit vs anti-Brexit), but each, in its own way, had broken down. Although, as always in Britain, there were some seats that were so strongly Labour or Tory that voters had, in effect, no choice, there were many constituencies where two other major parties (Liberal Democrats and Greens) were in contention, a situation complicated further in Scotland, Wales and Northern Ireland. There were also multiple positions in relation to Brexit: it was not just a question of supporting 'remain' or 'leave' since there were also many other variables, such as what kind of 'leave' deal to support, whether or not there should be a further referendum and so on.

This seems to have left many voters – significantly more than in previous elections – strongly conflicted about how to vote and feeling that there was no candidate who represented their views properly. It also created strong disincentives for parties to collaborate with each other.

Instead of being able to join forces around common views and platforms they were impelled by the situation to attack each other locally.

The third problematic dimension was how different versions of nationalism were played out in the debates, cutting across each other in ways that impeded rational dialogue. The xenophobic right-wing anti-European version expressed itself in the simple slogan 'get Brexit done', which was used to label any opposed view as anti-democratic (using referendum logic) and thus render any discussion of actual government policy irrelevant. Meanwhile, the left-wing 'socialism in one country' version proposed a detailed blueprint for an alternative way of running the country, in one of the most ambitious and radical manifestos ever produced by a British political party (a manifesto which, incidentally, overlaps to a considerable extent with the ideas proposed earlier in this book). However, the contradictory circumstances in which this manifesto was presented (helped along by biased media coverage) made it impossible for its contents to become the central debating point in the election campaign. Overwhelmingly, it seemed, voters' decisions were determined by other factors. So, instead of being about what sort of country UK citizens want to live in, the election became an expression of confusion and rage.

What can we learn from this experience? One obvious lesson is that there is a need for electoral reform and the introduction of some form of proportional representation. This does not just imply a need for different ways of campaigning and different forms of accountability by elected politicians, but also letting go of 'winner take all' fantasies that an entirely new political agenda can be introduced from scratch if a different political party takes power, because the chances are that proportional representation will lead, as it does in so many other European countries, to some form of coalition government. And coalition governments need to proceed by building consensus, which involves extensive discussion among the partners and reaching compromises that each of them can buy into. Purists will find this hard to take, but perhaps it is a lesser evil than being permanently out of office.

A second lesson is that capturing the national government, though a necessary precondition, is not a sufficient basis for bringing about effective change. In the context of globalisation it is also necessary to work with other governments at the supra-national level, and here too processes of discussion and negotiation and consensus-building become essential.

Thirdly, the election results, with their thumping Tory victory, suggest that the ensuing government may run for up to five years – five years in which continuing austerity policies, the terms of trade deals with the USA and yet more outsourcing may wreak havoc on what is left of our National Health Service and other aspects of the welfare state. If there is no scope to address this at the national level, then there is an urgent need to develop strategies to counter these trends at regional and local levels.

WHERE DO WE GO FROM HERE?

This is the analysis that informed the writing of this book. It starts by acknowledging the political dilemma facing anybody who wants to recreate a more equal society in Britain: that the national level is both crucially important and not enough. There are certain policies that have to be enacted at a national level to reverse the trends that have turned the welfare state into an inverted parody of what it was originally meant to be. I addressed some of these policies in chapters 5, 6 and 7, outlining proposals that could provide a basic scaffolding for a future welfare state. There are, of course, many more measures that would be required to cover the full range of government policies. I hope these suggestions can open up a discussion about what this future welfare state might look like that will inspire people to imagine it in detail, and begin to plan ways in which it might be brought into being.

Nevertheless, such discussions are unlikely in the short term to lead to any real change in national government policy, so I have tried to focus wherever possible on what can be done more immediately at a more local level. Even if they are not official national policy, there is scope for some of their elements to become the basis for voluntary codes of practice or administrative experiments at a city or regional level, or even a national level if the relevant authority has been devolved to Wales, Scotland or Northern Ireland.

Perhaps even more importantly, in the present context, there are many other possibilities for developing local experiments that could potentially improve the quality of life for local citizens, bringing about some redistribution to the households in greatest need, contributing to gender equality, countering the effects of austerity and some of the more penal aspects of the benefit regime, and reducing waste. Chapter 8 introduced some ideas to start the ball rolling here, using the potential of new platform technologies as a starting point.

Seeing online platforms as part of the solution to the problems that face us, in a country where working people have been impoverished and demoralised by the impacts of casualisation, privatisation and austerity, requires an effort of hope. It takes a major change in mindset to see these technologies not as a threat to the old welfare state model but as a means of rebooting it to make it fit for the twenty-first century. Using modern technologies to deliver services in new ways might change their form into something unforeseen but could, despite this apparent departure from tradition, bring them more closely into alignment with the original aim of the welfare state: to ensure that all citizens are provided with the basic services that enable them to live dignified, safe and healthy lives and bring up their children free from the threat of poverty.

It may also be hard to envisage the possibility that inventive uses of these technologies could help bring about the promise of women's liberation that has remained so elusive over the past seventy years. And it perhaps takes an even greater leap of faith to imagine that such uses might help us develop more environmentally friendly and less wasteful policies to tackle the threats to the sustainability of life on this planet.

Of course, none of these policies can deliver a revolution, but every little improvement to the living and working conditions of the local population helps, and every advance builds the confidence and political awareness to progress a bit further and demand more. In these despairing times, just restoring popular faith in local politicians is no mean achievement.

Any of these initiatives will need to start at the bottom, bringing people together from different institutions and different political parties to share ideas, brainstorm, plan and work out how to pool their resources for the common benefit. In coming together, openly and without a preordained agenda, perhaps these people will start to trust each other a little more and find ways to collaborate more deeply. Only such collective efforts can bring into being the twenty-first-century welfare state we need so badly.

Building new platforms and networks may seem daunting, but it falls into perspective when compared with the difficulties faced by the architects of our twentieth-century welfare state institutions. Just think of the challenges faced by Aneurin Bevan and his colleagues when they designed the National Health Service, in a context where infrastructure and many parts of the economy had been devastated by war, goods were rationed and, compared with what is available to us today, technology was primitive. If they could realise this grand vision – which, despite being battered savagely for much of its life, remains a hugely admired, loved and successful institution – then surely we, with the sophisticated technologies at our disposal, should be able to accomplish something comparable. Our children and grandchildren will hold us responsible if we fail to deliver it.

Notes

2 WHAT HAS HAPPENED TO THE TWENTIETH-CENTURY WELFARE STATE?

1. This dilemma was addressed in the Conference of Socialist Economists 1979 pamphlet *In and Against the State*: https://libcom.org/library/against-state-1979.
2. T. Miller and H. Pope, *The Changing Composition of UK Tax Revenues*, Institute for Fiscal Studies, 2016.
3. Private Finance Initiatives (PFIs) became popular in the 1990s under the New Labour government, as a means for large sums of money to be raised to pay for investment in state institutions such as schools and hospitals without taking the capital from public funds.
4. N. Davies, O. Chan, A. Cheung, G. Freeguard and E. Norris, *Government Procurement: The Scale and Nature of Contracting in the UK*, Institute for Government, 2018.
5. P. Gallagher, 'Virgin Care Services: no corporation tax paid as profits from NHS contracts rise to £8m on £200m turnover', *i*, 8 January 2018: https://inews.co.uk/news/health/virgin-care-no-corporation-tax-paid-profits-nhs-contracts-rise-8m-200m-turnover-515276.
6. 'Tax credits: how much has spending increased in 16 years?', *Fullfact*, 22 July 2015: https://fullfact.org/economy/tax-credits-how-much-has-spending-increased-16-years.
7. A. Armstrong, 'Amazon pays just £220m tax on British revenue of £10.9bn', *The Times*, 4 September 2019: www.thetimes.co.uk/article/amazon-pays-just-220m-tax-on-british-earnings-of-10–9bn-vv9fwxx52.

8. J. Lauerman, 'Starbucks paid 2.8 per cent effective U.K. tax last year, FT Reports', *Bloomberg*, 19 September 2018: www.bloomberg.com/news/articles/2018-09-19/starbucks-paid-2-8-effective-u-k-tax-last-year-ft-reports.

9. 'Steepest increase in people needing food banks for past 5 years as need soars by 23 per cent', Trussell Trust, 13 November 2019: www.trusselltrust.org/2019/11/13/april-sept-2019-foodbank-figures.

10. 'Rough sleeping: London figures hit record high', *BBC News*, 19 June 2019: www.bbc.co.uk/news/uk-england-london-48692703.

11. 'Personal Independence Payment: Written question – 203812', Hansard, 19 December 2018: www.parliament.uk/business/publications/written-questions-answers-statements/written-question/Commons/2018-12-19/203812.

12. A. Klair, 'Child poverty in working households has rocketed by 800,000 since 2010', TUC, 18 November 2019: www.tuc.org.uk/blogs/child-poverty-working-households-has-rocketed-800000-2010.

13. Office for National Statistics, *Living Longer: How our Population is Changing and Why it Matters*, 2016: www.ons.gov.uk/peoplepopulationandcommunity/birthsdeathsandmarriages/ageing/articles/livinglongerhowourpopulationischangingandwhyitmatters/2018-08-13.

14. 'Longer term influences driving lower life expectancy projections', Institute and Faculty of Actuaries, March 2019: www.actuaries.org.uk/news-and-insights/media-centre/media-releases-and-statements/longer-term-influences-driving-lower-life-expectancy-projections.

15. 'Do pensioners in the rest of the EU get more cash than the elderly in the UK?', *Fullfact*, 2018: https://fullfact.org/europe/pensioners-eu-uk/?utm_source=content_page&utm_medium=related_content.

16. B.B. Gilbert, 'Winston Churchill versus the Webbs: The origins of British unemployment insurance', *The American Historical Review* 71(3), 1966, pp. 846–62.

17. 'A century of change: Trends in UK statistics since 1900', House of Commons Library, 22 December 1999: https://researchbriefings.parliament.uk/ResearchBriefing/Summary/RP99–111; and '2011 census analysis: A century of home ownership and renting in England and Wales', National Archives, 19 April 2013: https://webarchive.nationalarchives.gov.uk/20160107120359/www.ons.gov.uk/ons/rel/census/2011-census-analysis/a-century-of-home-ownership-and-renting-in-england-and-wales/short-story-on-housing.html.

18. N. Sommerlad, 'Revealed: Britain's richest Tory MP collects £625k in tenants' housing benefits', Daily Record, 24 February 2014: www.dailyrecord.co.uk/news/politics/revealed-britains-richest-tory-mp-3177996.

3 WHAT HAS HAPPENED IN THE LABOUR MARKET?

1. I discuss this in more detail in U. Huws, N. H. Spencer and D. S. Syrdal, 'Online, on call: the spread of digitally organised just-in-time working and its implications for standard employment models', New Technology, Work and Employment 33(2), 2018, pp. 113–29.

2. Office for National Statistics, Dataset EMP17: People in Employment on Zero Hours Contracts, 12 August: www.ons.gov.uk/employmentandlabourmarket/peopleinwork/employmentandemployeetypes/datasets/emp17people inemploymentonzerohourscontracts.

3. J. Kollewe, 'Britain's agency workers underpaid and exploited, thinktank says', Guardian, 5 December 2015: www.theguardian.com/business/2016/dec/05/britains-agency-workers-underpaid-and-exploited-thinktank-says.

4. 'Record proportion of people in employment are home workers', National Archives, 4 June 2014: https://webarchive.nationalarchives.gov.uk/20160105210705/www.ons.gov.

uk/ons/rel/lmac/characteristics-of-home-workers/2014/
sty-home-workers.html.

5. Office for National Statistics, *Trends in Self-employment
   in the UK: 2001 to 2015*, 2016: https://www.ons.gov.uk/
   employmentandlabourmarket/peopleinwork/employment
   andemployeetypes/articles/trendsinselfemploymentin
   theuk/2018-02-07.

6. Under the umbrella contract system, temporary workers
   are set up as independent micro-companies, without
   employment status (and thus also without employment
   rights). A larger, specialist 'umbrella' company manages
   their accounts, including setting expenses such as travel
   costs against the company's 'profits'. Because of savings on
   national insurance and tax payments, these arrangements
   are made to seem attractive to workers, seeming to produce
   a higher average wage than temporary employment.

7. U. Huws (ed.) *When Work Takes Flight: Research Results
   from the EMERGENCE project*, IES Report 397, Brighton,
   2003, p. 24.

8. U. Huws, 'Where did online platforms come from? The
   virtualization of work organization and the new policy
   challenges it raises', in P. Meil and V. Kirov (eds) *The Policy
   Implications of Virtual Work*, London: Palgrave Macmillan,
   2017, pp. 29–48.

9. U. Huws, N.H. Spencer and M. Coates, *Platform Work in
   the UK 2016–2019*, Brussels: Foundation for European
   Progressive Studies, 2019: https://www.feps-europe.eu/
   attachments/publications/platform%20work%20in%20
   the%20uk%202016-2019%20v3-converted.pdf.

10. U. Huws, N.H. Spencer and M. Coates, *The Platformisation
    of Work in Europe: Highlights from Research in 13 European
    Countries*, Brussels: Foundation for European Progressive
    Studies, 2019: https://www.feps-europe.eu/attachments/
    publications/platformisation%20of%20work%20report%20
    -%20highlights.pdf.

11. Ibid.

12. K. Mitchell and J. Martin, 'Gender bias in student evaluations', *PS: Political Science & Politics* 51(3), 2018, pp. 48–652.

13. A. Rosenblat, S. Barocas, K. Levy and T. Hwang, 'Discriminating tastes: Customer ratings as vehicles for bias', *Data & Society*, October 2016, pp. 1–21.

14. H. Else, 'Academics "face higher mental health risk" than other professions', *Times Higher Education*, 22 August 2017: www.timeshighereducation.com/news/academics-face-higher-mental-health-risk-than-other-professions.

15. M. Taylor, G. Marsh, D. Nicol and P. Broadbent, *Good Work: The Taylor Review of Modern Working Practices*, London: Royal Society for the Arts, 2017: https://assets.publishing.service.gov.uk/government/uploads/system/uploads/attachment_data/file/627671/good-work-taylor-review-modern-working-practices-rg.pdf.

16. Ibid. pp. 8–9.

17. A. Ram, 'Taylor review member was early Deliveroo backer', *Financial Times*, 10 July 2017: www.ft.com/content/95392a68-6596-11e7-8526-7b38dcaef614

18. Taylor et al., *Good Work*, p. 35.

19. Ibid., p. 37.

20. See https://unitetheunion.org/media/1406/decent-work-for-all.pdf.

21. See www.bfawu.org/bfawu_mcdonalds_strike_press_release.

22. See https://notesfrombelow.org/issue/the-transnational-courier-federation.

23. See http://iaatw.org for more information.

24. Ben Tillot, *Dock, Wharf and Riverside Union: A Brief History of the Docker's Union*, London, 1910.

25. T. Mickle and P. Rana, 'These Airbnb hosts made "magical money." Now they're losing it all', *Wall Street Journal*, 29 April 2020; J. Faus, 'This is how coronavirus could affect the travel and tourism industry', *World Economic Forum with Reuters*, 17 March 2020: www.weforum.org/

agenda/2020/03/world-travel-coronavirus-covid19-jobs-pandemic-tourism-aviation.

26. U. Huws, 'Fixed, footloose, or fractured: Work, identity, and the spatial division of labor in the twenty-first century city', *Monthly Review* 57(10), 2006.

27. A. Holmes, 'Employees at home are being photographed every 5 minutes by an always-on video service to ensure they're actually working – and the service is seeing a rapid expansion since the coronavirus outbreak', *Business Insider*, 23 March 2020: www.businessinsider.com/work-from-home-sneek-webcam-picture-5-minutes-monitor-video-2020-3?r=US&IR=T.

28. U. Huws, *The Making of a Cybertariat: Virtual Work in a Real World*, New York: Monthly Review Press, 2003.

29. R.W. Aldridge, D. Lewer, S.V. Katikreddi, R. Mathur, N. Pathak, R. Burns, E.B. Fragaszy, A.M. Johnson, D. Devakmur, I. Abubakar and A. Hayward, 'Black, Asian and Minority Ethnic groups in England are at increased risk of death from COVID-19: indirect standardisation of NHS mortality data [version 1; peer review: 3 approved with reservations]', Wellcome Open Research, 6 May 2020: https://wellcomeopenresearch.org/articles/5-88/v1.

4   WHAT HAS HAPPENED TO GENDER EQUALITY?

1. Equal Pay Act: An Act to prevent discrimination, as regards terms and conditions of employment, between men and women, Parliament of the United Kingdom, 1970.

2. Equality and Human Rights Commission, *Fair Opportunities for All: A Strategy to Reduce Pay Gaps in Britain*, 2017, p. 4: www.equalityhumanrights.com/sites/default/files/pay-gaps-strategy-fair-opportunities-for-all.pdf.

3. M. Walsh, 'Womanpower: The transformation of the labour force in the UK and the USA since 1945', *Recent Findings of Research in Economic and Social History*, Summer 2001.

4. E. Altinas and O. Sullivan, 'Fifty years of change updated: Cross-national gender convergence in housework', *Demographic Research* 35(16), 2016, pp. 455–70.

5. International Labour Organization, *Care Work and Care Jobs: For the Future of Decent Work*, Geneva: ILO, 2018, pp. 44.

6. J. Gershuny, *Gender Symmetry, Gender Convergence and Historical Work-time Invariance in 24 countries*, Centre for Time Use Research, University of Oxford, 2018, p. 12.

7. H. Wallop, 'Million more people employ a cleaner than a decade ago', *Telegraph*, 1 July 2011: www.telegraph.co.uk/news/uknews/8608855/Million-more-people-employ-a-cleaner-than-a-decade-ago.html.

8. S. Poulter, 'Return of the cleaner: One in three families now pays for domestic help', *Daily Mail*, 31 March 2016: www.dailymail.co.uk/news/article-3516617/One-three-families-pay-cleaner-35s-drive-trend-hiring-domestic-help.html.

9. U. Huws, N.H. Spencer and M. Coates, *The Platformisation of Work in Europe: Highlights from Research in 13 European Countries*, Brussels: Foundation for European Progressive Studies, 2019: https://www.feps-europe.eu/attachments/publications/platformisation%20of%20work%20report%20-%20highlights.pdf.

10. Ibid.

5 RECALIBRATING THE MECHANISMS OF REDISTRIBUTION

1. 'Businesses demand more free childcare for workers', *Channel 4 News*, 10 November 2014: www.channel4.com/news/free-childcare-workers-business-britain.

2. W.H. Lewis, *The Power of Productivity: Wealth, Poverty and the Threat to Global Stability*, Chicago: Chicago University Press, 2014.

3. Ibid., p. xxiv.

4. See for example M. Sheffield, 'Poll: Majority of voters support $15 minimum wage', *The Hill*, 19 January 2020: https://thehill.com/hilltv/what-americas-thinking/426780-poll-a-majority-of-voters-want-a-15-minimum-wage.

5. Lewis, *The Power of Productivity*, 151.

6. Ibid., p. 16.

7. Ibid., p. 56.

8. A. Gray, C. Hampton, B. Jacobson, G. Morgan and M. Torry, *Universal Credit: Neither Universal nor Creditable*, London: Citizen's Basic Income Trust, 2020: https://citizensincome.org.

9. 'UK welfare spending: how much does each benefit really cost?', *Guardian*, 8 January 2013: www.theguardian.com/news/datablog/2013/jan/08/uk-benefit-welfare-spending.

10. H. Cottam, *Radical Help: How We Can Remake the Relationships Between Us and Revolutionise the Welfare State*, London: Virago, 2018, p. 39.

11. I discuss these and other such programmes in U. Huws, 'Saints and sinners: lessons about work from daytime TV', *International Journal of Media & Cultural Politics* 11(2), 2015, pp. 143–63.

12. M. Buchanan, 'Reality Check: How much benefit money is lost to fraud?', *BBC News*, 5 June 2017: www.bbc.co.uk/news/election-2017-39980793.

13. Office for Budget Responsibility, 'Tax by tax, spend by spend', 2019: https://obr.uk/forecasts-in-depth/tax-by-tax-spend-by-spend.

14. Gareth Morgan, 'National Living Wage: cui bono?', *Benefits in the Future*, 11 January 2020: https://benefitsinthefuture.com/national-living-wage-cui-bono.

15. House of Commons Library, *Education: Historical Statistics*, 2012: https://researchbriefings.files.parliament.uk/documents/SN04252/SN04252.pdf.

16. R. Adams, 'Almost half of all young people in England go on to higher education', *Guardian*, 28 September 2017: www.theguardian.com/education/2017/sep/28/almost-half-of-all-young-people-in-england-go-on-to-higher-education.

17. S. Connolly, 'Three-quarters of graduates will never pay off their student loans, finds report', *Independent*, 5 July 2017: www.independent.co.uk/student/graduates-three-quarters-never-pay-off-debt-loan-maintenance-grant-institute-for-fiscal-studies-a7824016.html.

18. A. McGettigan, *The Great University Gamble: Money, Markets and the Future of Higher Education*, London: Pluto Press, 2013.

19. S. Shackle, '"The way universities are run is making us ill": Inside the student mental health crisis', *Guardian*, 27 September 2019: www.theguardian.com/society/2019/sep/27/anxiety-mental-breakdowns-depression-uk-students

20. R. Murphy, 'Is VAT regressive and if so why does the IFS deny it?', *Tax Research UK*, July 12, 2010.

21. 'Government announces pay rise for 2.8 million people. National Living Wage set to increase by 6.2 per cent in 2020', 31 December 2019: www.gov.uk/government/news/government-announces-pay-rise-for-28-million-people.

22. M. Hart-Landsberg, 'Chart of the week: 1,500 estimates suggest a higher minimum wage will have no effect on jobs', *Sociological Images*, 3 January 2015: https://thesocietypages.org/socimages/2015/01/03/a-compilation-of-1500-estimates-suggests-that-raising-the-minimum-wage-will-have-zero-effect-on-employment.

6   A UNIVERSAL BASIC INCOME THAT IS GENUINELY REDISTRIBUTIVE

1. See R. Small, 'Silvia Federici reflects on wages for housework', *New Frame*, 18 October 2018: www.newframe.com/silvia-federici-reflects-wages-housework.

2. M. Torry, *101 Reasons for a Citizen's Income: Arguments for Giving Everyone Some Money*, Bristol: Policy Press, 2015.

3. See G. Morgan, 'Some typical household effects of a Citizen's Income scheme', Citizens Basic Income Trust, 21 September

2016: http://citizensincome.org/research-analysis/some-typical-household-effects-of-a-citizens-income-scheme; H. Reed and S. Lansley, *Universal Basic Income: An Idea Whose Time Has Come?*, London: Compass, 2016: www.compassonline.org.uk/wp-content/uploads/2016/05/UniversalBasicIncomeByCompass-Spreads.pdf; M. Torry, *Research Note: A Feasible Way to Implement a Citizen's Income*, Colchester: University of Essex Institute for Social and Economic Research, 2014: www.iser.essex.ac.uk/research/publications/working-papers/euromod/em17-14.

4. M. Torry, *Static Microsimulation Research on Citizen's Basic Income for the UK: A Personal Summary and Further Reflections*, Colchester: University of Essex Institute for Social and Economic Research, 2019, pp. 22ff: www.euromod.ac.uk/sites/default/files/working-papers/em13-19.pdf.

5. Ibid., p. 27.

6. 'The welfare budget', *Fullfact*, 10 July 2015: https://fullfact.org/economy/welfare-budget.

7. A. Bryson and J. Forth, *The Added Value of Trade Unions: A Review for the TUC of Existing Research*, London: TUC, 2017: https://www.tuc.org.uk/added-value-trade-unions.

7 A NEW DEAL FOR LABOUR

1. Employment Status Manual, 10 July 2010: www.gov.uk/government/publications/employment-status-manual.

2. K. Hughes, 'The hidden cost of self-employment', *Independent*, 25 October 2017: www.independent.co.uk/money/spend-save/self-employment-cost-holiday-pay-sick-leave-benefits-a8019171.html.

3. 'Two million self-employed adults earn less than the minimum wage', TUC, 28 September 2018: www.tuc.org.uk/news/two-million-self-employed-adults-earn-less-minimum-wage.

4. This is a rapidly changing situation, with cases and appeals going through the courts frequently. One of the

most comprehensive summaries can be found in J. Prassl, *Humans as a Service*, Oxford: Oxford University Press, 2018, but of course this must be updated in the light of ongoing judgements.

5. 'Uber London Limited found to be not fit and proper to hold a private hire operator licence', Transport for London, 25 November 2019: https://tfl.gov.uk/info-for/media/press-releases/2019/november/uber-london-limited-found-to-be-not-fit-and-proper-to-hold-a-private-hire-operator-licence.

6. See www.livingwage.org.uk/history.

7. See www.livingwage.org.uk/become-recognised-service-provider.

8. J. Manock, 'Manchester businesses pledge to ban zero-hours contracts', *Mancunion*, 31 January 2020: https://mancunion.com/2020/01/31/manchester-businesses-pledge-to-ban-zero-hours-contracts.

9. J. Halliday, 'Hull asks to be first UK city to trial universal basic income', *Guardian*, 19 January 2020: www.theguardian.com/uk-news/2020/jan/19/hull-universal-basic-income-trial. See www.ubilabnetwork.org.

10. Department for Business, Energy and Industrial Strategy (2019) *Good Work Plan: Establishing a New Single Enforcement Body for Employment Rights: Consultation*, July 2019: https://assets.publishing.service.gov.uk/government/uploads/system/uploads/attachment_data/file/817359/single-enforcement-body-employment-rights-consultation.pdf.

11. Ibid., p. 9.

12. See U. Huws, 'Working at the interface: Call-centre labour in a global economy', *Work Organisation, Labour and Globalisation* 3(1), 2009, pp. 1–8.

13. P. Bramming, O. H. Sørensen and P. Hasle, 'In spite of everything: Professionalism as mass customised bureaucratic production in a Danish government call centre', *Work Organisation, Labour and Globalisation* 3(1), 2009, pp. 114–30.

8   DIGITAL PLATFORMS FOR PUBLIC GOOD

1. H. Cottam, *Radical Help: How We Can Remake the Relationship Between Us and Revolutionise the Welfare State*, London: Virago Press, 2018.
2. Greater Manchester Health and Social Care Partnership, *Taking Charge in Greater Manchester – the Ambition for Primary Care*, 6 October 2016: www.gmhsc.org.uk/news/taking-charge-in-greater-manchester-the-ambition-for-primary-care.
3. For more on this, see M. Altenried, 'On the last mile: Logistical urbanism and the transformation of labour', *Work Organisation, Labour and Globalisation* 13(1), 2019, pp. 114–29.
4. C. Barbier, C. Cuny and N. Raimbault, 'The production of logistics places in France and Germany: A comparison between Paris, Frankfurt-am-Main and Kassel', *Work Organisation, Labour and Globalisation* 13(1), 2019, pp. 30–46.
5. T. Hayward, '"Dark kitchens" spell trouble for the restaurant trade', *Financial Times*, 29 March 2019: www.ft.com/content/755ddc1c-5obc-11e9-8f44-fe4a86c48b33.
6. Bristol Food Policy Council, *A Good Food Plan for Bristol*, November 2013: https://bristolfoodpolicycouncil.org/wp-content/uploads/2013/03/Bristol-Good-Food-Plan_lowres.pdf.
7. Interim Bristol Food Network, *A Sustainable Food Strategy for Bristol and Bristol Food Network*, 24 June 2009: www.bristolfoodnetwork.org/wp2/wp-content/uploads/2015/02/Sustainable-Food-Strategy.pdf.
8. Ibid., p. 2.
9. Department of Health, *Sustainable Food: A Guide for Hospitals*, 2009: www.sustainweb.org/pdf2/295087_sustainablefoodguide_acc.pdf.
10. See https://oxfordfoodbank.org.

Index

Thanks to our Patreon Subscribers:

Abdul Alkalimat
Andrew Perry

Who have shown their generosity and comradeship in difficult times.